John Burke

Chivalry, slavery, and young America

John Burke

Chivalry, slavery, and young America

ISBN/EAN: 9783744739528

Printed in Europe, USA, Canada, Australia, Japan

Cover: Foto ©ninafisch / pixelio.de

More available books at **www.hansebooks.com**

CHIVALRY SLAVERY,

AND

YOUNG AMERICA.

By SENNOIA RUBEK. *pseud*

NEW YORK:
FREDERIC A. BRADY, PUBLISHER,
No. 22 ANN STREET.
1866.

Entered according to Act of Congress, in the year 1866,
By JOHN BURKE,
in the Clerk's Office of the District Court of the United States for the Southern District of New York.

TO THE MEMORY

OF

RICHARD BURKE,

A VICTIM OF

KNOW-NOTHING AGITATION.

"*Non illo melior quisquam nec amantior æqui.*
"*Integer vitæ, scelerisque purus.*"

A WORD OF COMPLIMENT TO HIS ADOPTED COUNTRY.

"*Lectos ex omnibus oris
Enehis; et meritum, non quæ cunabula, quæris
Et qualis, non unde satus.*"

AUTHOR'S APOLOGY.

Now that Know-Nothingism is a thing of the past, that slavery is forever abolished in the United States, and that men's minds are chiefly occupied in the great work of reconstruction, it may be asked to what purpose is the publication of the following poems. The question, we think, is very easily and, we trust, satisfactorily answered. It will be readily conceded that the subjects to which these poems refer, are, like many other things of the past, still fresh in our remembrance, and not unworthy of being chronicled in verse or prose. If the author neglected to publish them, with such additions and improvements as time and opportunity have permitted, it is not at all improbable that they may, with many interpolations to his prejudice, be published at the South by his enemies, into whose hands, by the fortunes of war, they have fallen, with all his other manuscripts of thirty years' labor.

When, in the year 1864, the Author published in pamphlet form, and under a disguised name, a few poems, called the "Burden of the South," which now appear again in these volumes, he was, to his surprise, pressed with questions from various quarters regarding his birth, parentage, education, and calling, all which questions he declined to answer until the time arrived, if it ever should arrive, when it may be his fortune to publish something more important than the few pages of that little work. In anticipation, on the publication of these volumes, of inquiries similar to the above, the Author begs leave to inform his readers, that he has filled, for many years, an obscure, humble, but he trusts useful position, as a non-combatant in the military service of the United States. Having in the discharge of his duties to the Government, before the rebellion, contracted a fearful disease, he visited New York on leave of absence, with a view to the best surgical assistance. How he survived his sufferings is as much a mystery to himself as to others. More dead than alive, he lay for many days in a charity hospital, and reviving to consciousness, learned that the rebellion had commenced; that his property was in the hands of the rebels; his occupation gone; and that his family, like himself, in wretched health at the time, were flying before the enemy—on the prairies of the West—an Indian country—without even a blanket to cover them from the chilling vapors of the night.

AUTHOR'S APOLOGY.

Before his departure from Fort W——, he had, with his personal clothing, his manuscripts, and some curious and beautiful minerals, sent all his books, some of them rare and valuable works, to the care of the Quarter-Master at Fort Smith, Arkansas. All the information he has been able to obtain respecting them up to the present time, is, that they were turned over for examination to a committee, and that his writings in verse and prose, having been found full of treason to the South, books, papers, and all, were scattered among the inhabitants of that neighborhood. The loss of his cattle, which had greatly increased and multiplied in ten or twelve years; of his clothing, household furniture, and of every thing else he possessed, was as nothing to the Author in comparison with his papers and books, which he can never hope to replace, and which were the chief solace of his life.

A small carpet-bag contained all our worldly possessions, including crude copies of some portions of this work, when we arrived in New York. But let us speak in the third person. Here the Author, with a view to publication, visited some publishers and a few editors of the newspaper press. It must be borne in mind that he was poor, friendless, unknown, looking perhaps somewhat seedy, and was moreover diffident, sensitive, unassuming, humiliated, and well stricken in years. By some he was received and dismissed with curt courtesy, others were rude, abrupt, and insulting. There are who gave very bland advice touching slaves and slave-owners. He was damned with faint praise by a few, and by many most graciously ridiculed. At that time, and subsequently until a very recent period, he remembers no publisher—save Mr. G. P. Putnam, and the firm of Ticknor & Fields—to whose testimony he can refer with satisfaction. He is, however, a debtor to the wise and to the unwise, to the Greek and the Barbarian. Rejected as he was without examination, he had time to add, correct, and amend, and in regard to some of his manuscript to carry out literally the counsel of Horace "*nonum que prematur in annum,*" and so present to the public, for the most part, the well-matured fruit of his labor.

Should it interest any one to be acquainted with a little more of his personal history, be it known that after twelve months of poverty, sickness, and wretchedness, during which time he was incapable of discharging his duties, he was not forgotten by the War Department, but was restored to his former position, the duties of which, by no means onerous or irksome, he is now as well able to perform as at any former period of his life, and for which he is most thankful to the Almighty. The circle of the author's acquaintance in this part of the world is exceedingly limited. During his dark days of adversity he found, in the Rev. Dr. Ogilby of Trinity Church, a most kind, generous, and sympathizing friend; and during his illness derived much edification and instruction from the spiritual ministrations of the Rev. Dr. Muhlenbergh. To the Rev. Dr. Pyne of Washington

AUTHOR'S APOLOGY.

City he never can be sufficiently grateful. To General R. Marcy and his family, and the Chief of Artillery of the Army of the Potomac, General H. J. Hunt, whose heart and purse and influence were all at work in his behalf, he would vainly endeavor to express his obligations. From those faithful and excellent officers, General Martin Burke and General Harvey Brown, he has received marks of favor and consideration, which can never be forgotten; and always, and under all circumstances, from the Rev. Ralph Hoyt, of the Good Shepherd, the affectionate regards of a friend and a brother.

Churches of the Good Shepherd, in such statuary marble and dendritic rock as the writer of these lines discovered in his rambles through the Indian Territory, should be, were he a millionaire, erected in Fort Lee and Fifty-fourth street as testimonials more durable than brass of the Rev. Ralph Hoyt's Christian zeal and benevolence. He should also have a castle on his own grounds near the palisades, commanding a view of our commercial intercourse with a world only less extended than the range of his own philanthropy. For the Rev. Dr. Muhlenbergh S. R. would create a new department at St. Luke's Hospital in favor of those poor patients, whose habits, associations, physical condition, in short, whose idiosyncracies, of whatever kind, demand seclusion and privacy.

The author has now fought his battle of life, and finished his journey, or nearly so. He has nothing to ask save the restitution of his books and papers by the State of Arkansas, and of the general public such patronage of these little volumes as would enable him to pay the printer, which he is now endeavoring to do in part by monthly savings from a small income. With these two favors granted him the author would be perfectly contented, and rest in that peaceful security which nothing should ever take away.

SENNOIA RUBEK.

PREFACE.

A GOOD Satire upon our social, moral, religious, and political condition, as a people, is said, by our best reviewers, to be the chief *desideratum* in American literature. The shrewd Editor of the *New York Herald* has, under this impression, offered, within the last few days, Two Hundred Dollars ($200) for the best Poem, of four hundred lines or more, as a Satire upon the Follies of the day. He will doubtless have the satisfaction of drawing out many able and skilful writers, either as competitors for his prize, or for the sole honor of victory in such a contest.

We are said to be, touching satire—whether personal or general, individual or national—more thin-skinned than any civilized people, and this may account for the fact that so few good satires have appeared among us. But why we should be, in this matter, more sensitive than other nations, is a question of no very easy solution. There is so much to admire in our laws and institutions—so much that is wonderful in our progress in all the affairs of life, war, commerce, manufactures, agriculture, education, art, science, literature; our prosperity is so unbounded, our resources are so vast, and the increase of our population, native and foreign, so great and unexampled, that we ought to bear with more equanimity than

PREFACE.

any other community of mankind some wholesome reprehension, in verse or prose, of the peculiarities and eccentricities, the vaporing, conceit, and extravagance of many, very many, among us, and those, of course, the most untravelled and least enlightened of our citizens.

The great nations of antiquity were remarkably tolerant of satire, even when it dealt most severely with their own follies and vices. Horace, Terence, Juvenal, and Persius, among the Romans; among the Greeks, Lucian, Menander, and Aristophanes; in England, more recently, among our Anglo-Saxon cousins, Butler, Dryden, Pope, Swift, Donne, Young, Hall, Johnson, Wolcot, Hogarth, Byron, Hood, Jerold, Thackeray, Dickens; in France, Molière, Racine, Boileau, Corneille, Voltaire; in Spain, Cervantes; in Germany, Schiller, Goethe, Richter, have all satirized their countrymen, whensoever and wheresoever, in any station of life, they afforded them just cause of censure; nor did those authors by their satires ever forfeit their popularity as writers.

The Irish character, as satirized by Irishmen, is, in reference to their bulls and blunders, love and whiskey, wit, riots, wrath and blarney, a source of never-ending amusement to themselves and others. The Scotch take no offence at mocking imitations of their dialect, or sarcasms on their thrift and trimming, nor the English at our mimicry of Cockney pronunciation, or ridicule of their national pride or personal self-importance. On the contrary, they go much beyond us themselves in laughable exhibitions of vulgar slang, baseless assumption, and snobbish conceit. Of the truth of this remark, a few numbers of the *London Punch* will convince the most incredulous.

The effects of a good satire have often been felt through

PREFACE.

all the ramifications of society. De Foe says that national mistakes, vulgarisms, and even a general practice, have been reformed by a just satire. He has a remarkable passage against the Know-Nothings of his day in England, in consequence of their antipathy to foreigners, especially the Dutch, forgetting, as our natives do, their own descent from foreign ancestors :—

> " These are the heroes who despise the Dutch,
> And rail at new-come foreigners so much,
> Forgetting that themselves were all derived
> From the most scoundrel race that ever lived;
> A horrid crowd of rambling thieves and drones,
> Who ransacked kingdoms and dispeopled towns;
> The Pict and painted Briton, treacherous Scot,
> By hunger, thirst, and rapine hither brought;
> Norwegian pirates, buccaneering Danes,
> *Whose red-haired offspring everywhere remains;*
> Who, joined with Norman French, compound the breed,
> From whence your true-born Englishmen proceed—
> And lest, by length of time, it be pretended
> That climate may the modern race have mended,
> Wise Providence, to keep us as we are,
> Mixes us daily with exceeding care."

It cannot be denied that the subject of the present satire is of infinite importance to this country. A large party is, and always has been, opposed to foreign suffrage, or at least to the appointment of foreigners to places of trust in the State, and yet it has been clearly proved, by the late rebellion, that their loyalty to the Union has been greater by far than that of the native-born of all the States of the South, or than that of thousands at the North, and among them of many educated by the General Government at the Military Academy of the nation. The soldiers who served under Twiggs and Lynde *remained loyal to a man*, and I believe it is admitted that they were

PREFACE.

nearly all foreigners. The whole rebel army, in short, was, with few exceptions, composed of *natives*. As respects the Irish population, so much under the influence of Copperheads, in sympathy with rebels, and most inconsistently opposed to negro emancipation, I believe it is conceded that such of them as served in our armies, during the war, rendered as effective service to the Government as any other troops.

Though many imagine that Know-Nothingism is now dead, and not likely to be resuscitated, yet are there certain signs of the times, which would lead to the belief that "the snake is not killed, but scotched."

We may shock many deserving people by our animadversions on certain societies, but we only speak the honest conviction of our hearts, and repeat the lessons of experience, when we make bold to assert, that much of the apparent change of life, in many belonging to those societies, is occasioned by the substitution of *night drinking* for *open* indulgence *by day* in the use of intoxicating liquors. As respects the societies referred to, we need only add, that if Christianity does not make men good, sober, temperate citizens, no other affiliation can.

In relation to the word *Native* in this Poem, the author wishes it well borne in mind, that it is used altogether for convenience, as designating those Americans opposed to free labor, free suffrage, and eligibility to office of persons born in foreign States. It is not intended to apply to those born in the land who recognize in foreigners the rights and immunities guaranteed to all citizens by the letter and spirit of the American Constitution. The opposition to negro suffrage is based upon the fact of the negro's ignorance of the nature of the elective franchise. The same objection, of course, should lie against the equally ignorant of other races. If negroes must not enter into the waters of political life before they have learned to swim, we know not why others should be permitted to do so.

Of Indians, Fillibusters, and the Monroe Doctrine, the writer expresses his sentiments freely, fearlessly, unreservedly, and disinterestedly; nor does he doubt that the Editor of *The New York Herald* and others, from whom he differs *toto cœlo*, in some of his views, will weigh with candor his arguments, nor suffer a difference of opinion to bias their judgment as to the general merit of these satires.

SENNOIA RUBEK ascribes to Know-Nothing politics the untimely death of a most beloved brother, yet he disavows from his heart any sentiment that is unnational, unpatriotic, un-American, in the strictest and most comprehensive import of those terms; and in the hope and conviction that this assurance will be received in the same spirit of truth and candor in which it is now entertained and expressed, most respectfully submits his satires to the judgment of a liberal, discriminating, and enlightened public.

YOUNG AMERICA.

"Rumoris nescio quid."
CICERO.

Behold, ye are nothing, and your work is naught.
ISAIAH, xli.

ONE needs no pass-word nor degree,
True patriots to scan;
Their Talisman is Liberty,
Their Shibboleth is man.

CANTO I.

In an address to the Know-Nothings, the author contemplates, in connection with the loss of the elective franchise to foreigners, the abstraction of foreign labor and capital from all our institutions and possessions. Episode on the demoralizing influence of the Modern Drama. Our martyred President, and the Booth family. The Press. The Condition of our Streets. Cholera.

I.

YE blind "Vitruvii of Ruin!"
From Filmore to the lowest Bruin;
Who would from Foreigners withdraw
Their franchise rights conferred by law;
Take from our fields of golden grain,
Our blooming gardens' wide domain,
From flocks and herds now roaming wide,
O'er fertile meads and rivers' side,
Take from our cities as they rise—
Our temples reaching to the skies,
Our roads, our wharves, our harbors, fleets,
Our bridges, aqueducts, and streets,
Our tunnels, railways, barges, locks,
Our steamers, merchantmen, and docks—

Take from our furnaces and looms,
Our quarries, mines, our hamlets, homes,
Our stores, our shops, our trains of cars,
Our camps, our fortresses, bazaars—
The labor wrought by foreign hands,
Their produce, capital, and lands!
Ah, me! the foreign bones and dust—
Cemented with our public works;
Would, if erected as a bust,
Or mound as wont among the Turks;
Or, say enclosed within an urn—
For States there be which corpses burn—
A bust, a mound, an urn, a frame,
Require as large as any name,
Among the Pyramids; which came
From most remote antiquity!
But *thanks* for foreign blood or bone,
Or crushed by weight of log or stone,
For money spent or labor done—
In any service, *e'en their own*—
To *natives* is *iniquity!*

II.

Take from our colleges and schools
Books, teachers, lessons, foreign rules—
From all our union trades and arts,
What foreign influence imparts;
Take from our press its foreign force,
Its every foreign help and source
Of knowledge, profit, power,
Prints, foreign papers, and reviews,
Our weekly, daily foreign news—
Writers, reporters, carriers take,
Let foreign editors forsake
Their chairs forevermore.

Take from our operas and balls,
Our orchestras, theatres, halls,
Their music, dresses, scenery.
But *that* you *can't*—a people used
To foreign shows, will be amused,
Though often to their cost abused
By humbug and chicanery!
Ay, more than humbug, gracious God,
Why should our scenic boards be trod
By the worst brotherhood of vice
From every land's metropolis?
Not thus was sought the Grecian stage,
That mirror of a golden age,
When myriads entered at its gates,
And thronged its high ascending seats,
To hear the tragic muse proclaim
Their country's valor, power, and fame;
Nor less when with the magic art
Of genius, Roscius reached the heart
Of Roman citizens, and found,
In answering echoes all around,
That vice unfigleafed shrunk and sought
In vain to shun the light that brought,
In fiercest wrath and darkest hue,
Its hateful image to the view;
Yet Rome's theatrical renown
Must yield to Greece the tragic crown.
Not so the British muse: in all
Her tragic scenes, or comical,
Or mimic, or satirical;
Our glorious Shakspeare stands confest,
Above the greatest and the best
Of Greece, or Rome, or France or Spain,
And so for ever will remain.
Yet he, in sunshine or in storm

So true to nature, needs *reform*.
Behold the Drama now disgraced
By robbers, bullies, bawds, and paste,
Fescennine masks and vulgar gibes,
And all the progeny of bribes,
With brazen front displayed, as once
In revolutionary France,
Or in that shame of British Isles,
The stygian purlieus of St. Giles,
To extirpate the moral sense
Of blooming youth and innocence.
When not received as thieves and rogues,
As robbers, murderers, and Thugs,
But decked with plumes and civic wreaths,
Our Turpins, Sheppards, and Macheaths,
Are, in theatres and saloons,
Enacting villains and buffoons—
All hailed with long and loud applause,
As heroes unrestrained by laws;
Why marvel that our lanes and streets,
Our offices and home retreats,
Are so beset by depredators,
Cut-purses, murderers, garotters,
Seducers, swindlers, siren-cells,
Drabs, drunkards, gamblers, brothel hells,
That some apprentices and clerks,
Like vultures or voracious sharks,
To glut their appetite for pleasure,
Should each, according to his measure,
Lay hands on his employer's treasure;
Why marvel such a set of fellows
Should stage our jails and star the gallows.

Stage-plays, and characters so fraught
With lewdness, both in act and thought,

And word and look, and unchaste dress,
The garb of impish bawdiness,
Demands an outcry from the press;
Nor let its strictures be in vain,
This Thespian license to restrain,
Lest other Presidential murders
Be added to our foul disorders.

Our martyred Lincoln from on high
Looks down with ever-pitying eye
Upon our inconsistency.
Ah! where is now the grief which late
Pervaded every realm and state?
Nay, every village, house, and home,
Within the bounds of Christendom,
And far beyond; for Moslem tribes
Send forth their orators and scribes,
Their heartfelt sympathy to show
In strains responsive to our woe.
Nor less do Brahma's followers own
Our people's loss, our chief's renown.
Yet in the city where his hearse—
The wonder of the universe—
In solemn and funereal state,
With more than royal splendor great,
Drew tears from eyes unused to weep,
And from our pillows banished sleep,
Men rush in crowds to greet and hear
The brother of his murderer!
Is this the gratitude we feel,
And this the faith our acts reveal,
In him whose consecrated blood,
Cementing human brotherhood,
Of varying type and caste and shade,
As by creative wisdom made,

Became a costly sacrifice
For national iniquities!
O cruel! cruel! cruel lot!
To be thus speedily forgot
By those who should his high deserts
Embalm within their heart of hearts!
To him it was reserved to strike
The cursed chain from slavery's neck,
To make the bondman taste and see
The priceless fruits of liberty,
And at her shrine the homage pay
Of nations ransomed in a day.
Cease Edwin Booth! to show thy face in
The character of an assassin!
At least ne'er venture to appear
In Sophoclean buskin here,
Where memory in thine every feature
Seeks traces of thy brother's nature;
And some with curses long and loud
Denounce the hated brotherhood.
Thy brother's keeper, true, thou wert not,
And an approver, doubtless, art not,
Of his offence, which smells to heaven,
A crime too rank to be forgiven;
But though thou didst not in his guilt
Take part, the blood so foully spilt
Will stain the records of thy name
Through all its calendar of fame.
This only copperheads deny,
Thy vanity to gratify;
Or on their party schemes intent,
To use thee as an instrument.
A fickle multitude may go,
As they are wont, to any show;
But those who wish to see thee most,

YOUNG AMERICA.

In fancy hear poor Lincoln's ghost,
Like Hamlet's, everywhere around,
Or see him dying of the wound
Inflicted by that cursed hand
Which smote the mirror of our land.
Suppose Wilkes Booth had killed the son,
Wife, brother, sire, of any one
Who now is nightly found among
The crowds that to thine acting throng;
Think'st thou he would thy presence greet
At every play, in every street,
Nor rather wish and pray and hope
To see thee dangling from a rope?
Why then, when our chief magistrate—
The ruler of a mighty state—
Is slain, why should our people cheer
The brother of his murderer?
Dramatic rant and fitful ire
And drunken brawls disgraced thy sire;
What marvel then, that, wedded so,
His spouse brought forth a child of woe
And wrath and shame and monster vices,
Increased by scenic artifices?
Such all must needs admit in sooth
Was the assassin, John Wilkes Booth.

Not tears alone and doleful cries
Characterize our Tragedies,
But *blood*, which, found in every age
A feature of the British stage,
May in some hearts those passions nurse
That prove a hissing and a curse.
In keeping with thy first intent
Of voluntary banishment,
Retire with ample means and ways

To spend thy residue of days
In private life, admired, esteemed,
And as a loyal burgess deemed.
The gods may now with loud applause
Greet thee, yet reason finds just cause,
E'en though the pit should also cheer,
To damn thee in thy pet career.

As faithful watchmen keeping guard
In every town and city ward,
Our daily journals now proclaim
The burdens of a grievous shame,
Of seething filth and festering stews
In cellar-tenements and mews;
And garbage, slush, and foul disease,
And all the steams and stench of vice,
Of bone-house caldrons, putrid flesh,
And heaps of decomposing fish;
Of sess-pools, shambles, tanneries,
Pest-houses, hells, infirmaries,
And want, and poverty, and woe,
And all the ills that overflow,
To taint the air and choke the breath,
Like poison from a den of death:
Such scenes must every feeling shock
In hearts not harder than a rock.
If now upon the Simoom's blast
Grim death, careering from the east,
Should, in the shape of cholera,
His ever-dreadful visit pay;
Such the condition of our streets,
Our sewers, sinks, and other seats
Of filth, our slaughtered populace
Would in our catacombs lack space.
Then would the curse of dead men's eyes

Pursue our street authorities,
, Our city council and their tools,
Now self-condemned as erring fools;
And worse than fools, a set of knaves
Whose hell begins this side their graves.
Return we now, again to pay
Our dues to *Young America.*

III.

Take what is foreign from our codes,
Of laws and manners, forms and modes,
In medicine what we may obtain—
From foreign sources let remain.
  In darkness and in night—
What foreign literature has taught—
Let us eschew, some think it fraught
  With *anti-slavery light.*

IV.

And so it is, for we suppose,
That all who write in verse or prose,
If they be honest, must condemn
That ruthless, heartless class of men,
Who deal in human flesh and blood,
As those who purchase daily food.
We cannot censors now elect,
Books to approve and to reject—
Broadcast, the press, in bales and billions,
Sends out those works which please the millions;
The leaven of freedom in our schools
Spreads slowly, yet, by certain rules,
Which find a suitable expression
In arithmetical progression;
As in our geologic laws,
We trace each layer to its cause:

Wave after wave, deposing matter,
As the condition of the water;
Or those phenomena of nature—
Volcanoes, earthquakes, mark each feature.
So, in the wavelets of the mind,
We may some certain traces find,
With now and then "a fault or dike,"
Which mark the bounds and show the extent
Of progress in each great event,
Or past or present, which, belike,
May operate in future ages,
In the same ratio of stages,
Till men obey each law divine,
As nature in the hidden mine.
And every man in every other
May view an equal and a brother,
Perfecting thus pure freedom's code,
To man delivered by his God.

V.

Let Milton, Spenser, Shakspeare lie
With Dryden, in obscurity,
And Goldsmith, Byron, Moore, and Young,
And Scotia's sweetest child of song—
Immortal Burns, whose fame is not
One whit behind the fame of Scott—
Send Wordsworth, with his angelot,
Divine philosophy to quote
To eagles, choughs, and rocks—
Show Southey, Coleridge, Bowles the way—
With epic, sonnet, German play
To line a trunk or box.
Pope, Campbell, Rogers, send them where
Macaulay's left to rot.

CANTO II.

Treats briefly of our obligations to men of science in the mother countries. What we owe to France, Germany, Italy. A Mammoth Skeleton—Babylon or Rome not so great a mass of ruin.

I.

Of sons of science we might name,
Conspicuous in the rolls of fame,
A host of men whom Britain gave,
But we our privilege shall waive;
And simply ask who first made known
The laws which rule the sun and moon—
The laws, whose heaven-directed force,
Maintains the planets in their course?
Who traced their orbs through endless space,
Their sizes, figures, distance, place?
Who taught whence they derived their light,
Whence their velocity of flight?
Who first, with scientific ken,
Gauged their diameters; and when
The cycles of their days and moons,
Their seasons, years, their nights and noons,
Expire: Why Cynthia's golden horn
Wanes, waxes, disappears at morn,
And why, at night, she reappears,
A queen among the troops of stars,
Which all, in pure and bright array,
Around her throne their homage pay!
Who taught how comets in their course,
Revolving with elliptic force—
At certain periods come and go—
Portending wrath and overthrow,
As some suppose, to mighty States,
When doomed to ruin by the fates?

II.

See Nature's Bible, writ in stone,
In short, in all we gaze upon—
See revelation, nor be loth,
The self-same source to claim for both,
Dividing sunshine from the night—
Or darkness from celestial light—
The light of truth: Or, call it day,
Of Heaven, an uncreated ray—
Day unto day revealing more
Than ever was revealed before;
And night to night more useful knowledge
Than ever was acquired at college.
Thy beams, Geology! at morn,
With glorious light our land adorn.
We rank in thee "no whit behind"
The oldest nations of mankind;
Or, if in aught, perhaps the style
Of Miller, Connybeare, and Ly'll.

III.

In Humboldt, Goëthe, Schiller, see,
Those noble lights of Germany;
See Gesner, Leibnitz, and Des Cartes—
Where'er philosophy and art
      Have spread their fame afar.
La Lande, La Place, and Carnot next,
May furnish each a glorious text
      For science and for war.
Guizot, Thiers, and Lamartine,
Arago, Cuvier, I ween,
Will scarcely be displaced by those
Who would not lead men by the nose,

To think all learning but their own,
A burden and excrescence grown.
Italian names would far extend
Our rhymes beyond what we intend,
Especially in works of art :—
We therefore with our reader part
On this point; promising again
To touch on painting, sculpture, when
We find what's written is disputed,
Or these, our present rhymes, refuted.

IV.

Remove all works, nor let remain
Aught, but what *Natives* may attain,
    Without external aid;
Then, if you can, with steadfast gaze,
Behold the ruin you have made,
Of genius, wisdom, strength, and health,
In this our glorious Commonwealth.
Behold! I write it with amaze—
A lifeless mammoth skeleton,
Of withering muscle, nerve, and bone—
    Destruction all around!
The fearfullest and wildest sprite,
That ever glared on mortal sight,
    Or uttered doleful sound!
A hydra corse! a Saurian home!
A second Babylon or Rome.
    Low levelled with the dust,
A constellation, chaos turned—
A world of light, in darkness mourned,
    A monumental crust,
Of all that was both good and great,
The nurse of thought and free debate,

In this fair orb of man's abode,
His fairest, brightest, best estate,
Next paradise and God.

CANTO III.

Many Foreigners supposed to be quite as competent to exercise their elective franchise rights, for the public good, as thousands of our *Know-Nothing Natives*. Morally, and in other respects, as good men as those who choose a booby name. Certain Secret Societies in league with Know-Nothings. One such Society described. Symbols and Watchwords a Sham. Election Days. Pat, Teague, Donald, Crapaud, and Snyder. A broad view of depravity in *Natives* and Foreigners. From Oregon to Maine, &c. Why should a test be required of one class of bad men and not of another?

I.

IF, of the millions native born,
Who view a foreigner with scorn,
There were not thousands, who, in worth,
To thousands yield of foreign birth,
A few of *these*—it may be so—
For we protest, we do not know—
Might *then* despairingly forego
    Their rights, and sink to slaves.
And if some myriads may be found,
From foreign peoples all around,
    As wise, as good, as just,
As some who choose a booby name,
To hide the acts which fear or shame
    Compel them to distrust:
Should we a difference seek to make—
Reject the good, and freemen take
    From villains and from knaves?
Who constitutions sets at naught,
Who puts up conscience to be bought;

Who auctions places for the wage
Of highest pay for meanest gage;
Who musters factions in the State,
For anarchy and civil hate;
Who has no barrier in laws,
Who views the person, not the *cause*,
Who dares invade his neighbor's right
By tests and theologic spite;
Nay: who for party, clamor, hire,
Would even disfranchise his own sire!
Pray, is not such a one, in truth,
Less Christian, citizen, and man—
    Though in our country born—
Than who, because of change or chance,
May not among us pass his youth—
But whom the State would fain advance,
Who would, though under *native ban*,
    The highest place adorn?

II.

And ye with titles meet for gibes,
Grand, worthy Pharisees and Scribes,*

---

* It is impossible to exaggerate the evils of drunkenness. Temperance Societies, so called, cannot prevent or do away with it. They only diminish it in appearance, or change its character, by substituting hypocrisy and night drinking for open and shameless intemperance. Those societies have degenerated into mere political clubs—the hybrids of a hybrid Odd-Fellowship. They have constituted themselves, with signs and symbols, into the most pragmatical and inquisitorial of all secret fraternities. Smellers and peepers, as they are frequently termed, they excite the disgust and indignation of every manly and generous spirit.

Be it emphatically understood, that it is not the cause of temperance we condemn. Heaven forbid! but those pretenders to temperance, whose rules and whose practice, so much at variance, have produced, now produce, and will con-

Even to yourselves a mockery!
To us poor laics, it appears,
That velvet feet and trumpet ears
Should to such animals belong,
As lie in wait to catch their prey,
Which first they sport with ere they slay,
   The jungle roots among.
No eagle, vulture, lynx, or kite,
Can match you in the sense of sight;
No hound or setter-dog excel
Your houndless faculty of smell,
Whene'er through crevices and chinks
You seek the seats of baneful drinks;
Or in the breeze, or on the breath,
Perceive the taint of moral death,
   In alcoholic cookery!

III.

Ye lights in darkness! normal schools!
Guides of the blind, instructing fools!
Ye have of knowledge but the form—
Your heart of hearts a canker-worm
Devours, as locusts oft are seen
Devouring whatsoe'er is green.
When warping from a leeward shore,
They on our crops their legions pour;
The skeletons of herbs and plants
They leave to beetles, grubs, and ants,

---

tinue to produce, a reaction, that is calculated to plunge men more and more into cant, profligacy, servility, and incurable meanness. Admitting that the ancient Masonic and other Societies—apart from strictly religious ones—have done good, yet we assert, without fear of contradiction, that they are not necessary, and that one great society, the Christian Church, of which all should be members, can alone be the means of "uplifting our humanity from its deep degradation."

As all good locusts for a feast
Must have what food they can digest.
Our laws and freedom thus bereft—
The spirit gone, the letters left;
Nor this left all—a shell, a frame—
Grand worthy scribes record your shame,
Your double infamy proclaim.
    You, kind inquisitors, forsooth!
Domestic foibles to detect,
    Advise the aged, save the youth,
And from strange gods the land protect!
Look well at home, you need not roam,
    For lives that want reform;
Your heart presents the elements
    That typify the storm.
By you society is batched
Into the watching and the watched;
"A thief to catch a thief," of course,
Your maxim, ever in full force.
Detectives all—a scurvy set—
As ever yet in conclave met;
Foes of all truth and independence:
Who, from one word, concoct a sentence,
And from one sentence coin a speech:
Some honest record to impeach.
Yea, from imaginary evil,
Are ready to stir up the Devil;
For instance, in the smell of wine,
To find unpardonable sin;
And oft, without a shade of reason,
Accuse a brother of high treason
To every pure and sacred code
Of laws, enjoined by man and God.
You, honest patriots, indeed!
You men whose sordid, selfish greed—

Whose every wish and end and aim
Is place and pension, power and fame;
Ay! pelf the means and power the end,
To which your signs and pass-words tend.
Your meddling, prying, knavish tricks,
All meet in party politics;—
No more with oaths and symbols vain,
The name of patriot profane.
One needs no pass-word nor degree,
   True patriots to scan;
Their Talisman is *Liberty*,
   Their *Shibboleth* is *Man*.

IV.

'Tis true, that on election-day,
Pat puts his spade and shou'l away,
And trudges to record his vote,
With stammering tongue and tattered coat,
With broken head and battered nose,
And other signs of cuffs and blows;
That Teague and Donald have their fill,
And old Crapaud his wonted swill,
   On great days of the feast;
And that mine vriend, our goot mynheer,
May pour a quart of horrid beer
   On stomach filled with crout,
And, without fear of God or law,
With neighbor or his comely frau,
   A rumpus raise or rout,
   And make himself a beast!
But do they more than others do,
Who, better taught, ought better know,
   A pure and perfect way?
Our guardian watchmen are not lulled,
Nor penal statutes disannulled,

By gross but partial ill,
Protective laws and justice still
Their aim and object to fulfill:—
Defend the weak, subdue the strong,
Prohibit violence and wrong,
    And punish whom they may.

v.

Yet, look abroad with map in hand—
Survey at large our mighty land—
Look this way, westward from Cape Fear,
Tow'rd Rio Grande, far as Mier,
Thence passing up to Santa Fé,
Or if you will, Francisco Bay;
Or, say we go to Utah Lake,
A close reconnoissance to make
    Of Mormon lust and blasphemy;
Or of the California schools
Of politics and moral rules,
    And all their Lynch-law infamy;
Or, of the hells and of the mines
Take views from Devil's Mount;*
Or, like the student in Le Sage,
Through every roof the living page
    Of every life recount—
    Men's virtues and their sins:
Think you that in this mighty space
We may not find a full-grown race,
    Of *natives born free*,
As vicious, villanous, and vile
As e'er, from continent or isle,
    Abused the name of Liberty?

---

* Monte Diavolo.

Alas! who travels on our coast,
  Who can a native riot see?
  Whose home's a city, village, town,
    Plain, mountain, backwood, parts unknown,
Yet shut his eyes and proudly boast,
  Of our supreme morality?
Poll foreign ruffians most forlorn—
Each villain also native born—
Each thief, each swindler, traitor, knave
  Of high or low degree;
All who, in short, to vice enslave
  The spirit's immortality:
Their crimes and ignorance compare—
  Their number, too, and then declare
Why worth, which you would make a test,
  When foreigners ask equal right,
You hold no better than a jest
  When native claims are brought to light?

VI.

But you don't mean to disfranchise
The good, intelligent, and wise;
You only mean to show good cause
For change in our organic laws—
  Restricting freedom's boon.
In short, you think it meet and just
That posts of profit, power, and trust
  Should only be to natives given;—
"Americans this land must rule,"
The maxim of the native school—
  You think a voice from Heaven!

CANTO IV.

Shows who is not a true American. Treats of the Louisville Riots. A trio of Editors, all of whom are Fillibusters, and two of them Know-Nothings.

1.

SHALL we Americans call those
Who disregard the countless woes
Of war in every race or nation,
With or without civilization?
Or the aggressive Fillibuster,
Who would his hireling ruffians muster,
To rob and steal from love of pelf,
And sole aggrandizement of self;
Who values not a single straw
Or life, or liberty, or law;
Or doctrines of a Whig or Tory,
Or faith, or our Republic's glory;
Albeit his lying tongue may wag
Of ceaseless insults to our flag.
Nor more American is he,
  Who, by brute violence, abuses
The man that uses liberty
  To vote for whomsoe'er he chooses.
Not muffled daggers, pistols, oaths,
Nor foul blaspheming funnel mouths,
Nor well-directed salivation,
Nor anti-despot declamation,
Nor Anglican vituperation,
Nor over-reaching the unwary;
  Nor aught that's rude in speech or dress,
Although perhaps they are not chary
  In plain distinctness to express
Their sentiments, can ever mark
Our true Americans. But hark!

YOUNG AMERICA.

What frantic noise invades our ears—
What shrieking, wailing, bitter crying?
Men, women, children, bleeding, dying!
Houses on fire! and, borne on biers,
At every turning-point, one meets
The dead and wounded in our streets.
Alas! alas! between the fire
   Of their own dwellings and the range
   Of fierce assassins' deadly rifles,
The aged matron, hoary sire,
The child, the youth, the maid expire.
   In one sad hour, ah! what a change
   Can ruthless ruffians make from trifles!
Yet not Americans are men
Who gag the press, who bribe the pen—
Ascribe to foreign peoples *all*
The human evils which befall
   In populations, *where, alas!*
They often *share* in evil-doing—
Their opportunities foregoing,
Of cultivating peace, good-will,
   With every citizen and neighbor,
As well as exercising skill
   In every art, in every class
   Enriched and honored by their labor.

But these things admitted, we cannot be blind
To the frenzy possessing the popular mind.
Ye sons of Kentucky, so gallant and brave,
To strangers so kind, and so good to the slave—
Abroad so esteemed, so respected at home,
From Cadiz to Glasgow, from Moscow to Rome,
From Maine to Panama, ay! farther, in truth—
Where bounds Colorado the plains of the South,*

---

* P. S. means that Rio Colorado which, flowing through the southern pampas

YOUNG AMERICA.

Why should the voice of a Know-Nothing press
To strangers and foreigners cause such distress ?
Some journals among you, confessedly *clever*,*
Keep credulous crowds in a crisis of fever—
Of principles judging by *stubborn facts*,
And these ('tis so said), by authentical pacts—
A bribe, in the guise of a generous loan,
A Cerberus sop, or a meat-covered bone,
An office to build, or a press to renew,
Will greatly contribute to alter one's view;
A diamond to wife, or to child, a rich present,
To *some*, as *douceurs*, are amazingly pleasant;
Such things made the greatest of orators dumb—
He had swallowed *gold cups* and could only say *mum!*†
Gold buttons, rare diamonds, rich cabinet wares,
Led Verulam's lord into troubles and snares.‡

---

of Buenos Ayres, falls into the Atlantic Ocean some miles south of the Bay of Anegarda, about 38¼ S. lat.

* " Do you mean *English* clever or *American* clever?" shouted a critic in the ear of S. R., as he uttered that word. " Look to the context," replied the satirist. I write *English.*

† For the story of the bribery of Demosthenes, see Plutarch. " Demosthenes could not resist the temptation—*i. e.*, of the gold cup and twenty talents. He received the money like a garrison into his house, and went over to the interest of Harpalus. Next day he came into the assembly with a quantity of wool and bandages about his neck, and when the people called upon him to get up and speak, he made signs that he had lost his voice. Some answered, ' By *swallowing gold and silver !*' At another time, when he wanted to speak in his own defence, somebody or other stood up and said, sneeringly, ' *Will you not hear the man with the cup ?*' "

‡ Without entering into the over-nice distinction between *Vitia temporis* and *Vitia hominis*—a plea on which many, besides Lord Bacon, might set up some defence—we take, as evidence of his guilt, his own humble confession to the lords, &c., in which he says: "I do plainly and ingenuously confess that I am guilty of corruption, and do renounce all defence, and put myself on the grace and mercy of your lordships." See Life and Works of Lord Bacon, pp. 96, 97; see, also, 3d, 9th, and 19th articles of charge.

Another example than either, much worse,
Is Judas, with silver and gold in his purse!
Gold often occasions a chronic bronchitis,
The brain it congeals and disorders the wit;
The *bright* it makes *murky*, the *lynx-eyed makes fit*
To *stumble* in *mire* or *fall* into a *pit*.
Men scarcely *know why*, and they cannot *tell when*,
The spirit of change has come over their *pen—*
A change of that sort so confoundedly *fleet is!*

There is, if he could, who, foul murder excusing,
The guilty defending, the victim abusing,
Would fain prove the heart of a sparrow-legged cripple
As soft as a mole-skin, and pure as a ripple
On Heaven-fanned waves of the waters of life—
Better prove from his *book* his aversion to strife.
How, spitting above and below and around him,
He would worry a Briton and try to impound him;
From John so familiar with costard and face,
With impudent boasting and monkey grimace;
If striking such reptile were not a disgrace
(Such cases excepted as that of poor Butler,*
Whose doom was forecast in the shop of a cutler);
Our cripple in limb but in spirit a thug,
Might catch some mischance o'er the site of his plug.

---

* See a book called "English Items," by Matt. Ward, a very sink of hatred, malice, and envy. It was avowedly designed as a set-off against the Trollopes and Fidlers of their day, and in acrimony and malignity, in all, in short, but ability, went far beyond them. When a certain by-stander had heard a young friend of S. R. read a few passages from the book referred to, he exclaimed: "Surely the fellow who wrote that book will *commit murder before he is six months older!*" Alas, alas! not more than six days had elapsed from that time, when the newspapers had informed the most distant parts of our Union, that poor *Butler's wife was a widow and his child an orphan!*

YOUNG AMERICA.

At home among cousins, such brutalized pranks
Would end in their smashing his teeth or his shanks.*
Ye shades of the murdered! if shade ever sent is!
Appear and refute the assertions of * * * * * * * *!

If murder again be committed, regard him
Who looks to an advocate's fee to reward him!
Who won't all free voters, who clash with, or *rat* him,
To kill to the war-cry of "*Up, Guards, and at them!*"
Who, if you would catch a political fish,
Will *echo* Buchanan with *cries* of *Buksheesh*—
Like Pat, who to "*How d'ye's?*" in Sullivan's dell,
Is answered by *Echo:* "*I thank you, sir, well!*"
He greedily gulps a gold bait with the hook!
Not Pat, but our man of the gudgeon and fluke—
For *money* he *will* have, by *hook* or by *crook*,
By *lecture*, by *libel*, by *song*, or by *wit*,
By *puffing*, *derision*, *black mail*, or deceit.
A man ever ready to taunt or proscribe him,
Who is not a "*Native*," or scorns to bribe him,
He seems to expect, as the meed for his crimes,
(This multiple multiplied echo of chimes)—
A flattering notice or two in the *Times*.†

---

* One of the witnesses in Ward's trial, for the murder of Butler, spoke of Ward's legs as the smallest and feeblest he had ever seen. What a fellow to seek quarrels with John Bull; and, ye gods, what a representative of John Mammoth! Physical infirmities, are, we freely admit, no legitimate subject for satire, unless (as we devoutly believe they are, in the cases of Ward and Prentice) the cause or effect, or both, of great moral depravity. Considering its own savage attacks upon some of the most venerable characters in Christendom, there is no newspaper in existence that has less reason to complain of the severity of satire than the *Louisville Journal*.

† The influence of the London *Times* upon public opinion in this country, as everywhere else, is wonderful; but, considering its far-seeing views upon political bearings and events, the pith and point of its leaders, and the unsurpassed ability

YOUNG AMERICA.

The *Times*, in the van of an era of mind,
Its influence happily wields for mankind;
Its thundering peals and electrical force,
To stay or to hasten or alter the course
Of events, in the march of an empire or state,
All seem to promulgate the fiats of fate.
(Ah me! what a change in foreknowledge and merit
Has lately come o'er its political spirit!)
Other journals, as planets, were lost in its blaze,
Or asteroids hid in a nebulous haze,
The hope to be mentioned with praise in its columns,
With P—— outweighs a *whole score of their volumes;*
Our native laudation is scarcely a puff
In the vanes of a kite, whose soul cry is "*luff, luff!*" *
His hatred of Catholics—German or Irish—
Is wolfish, malignant, as cruel as CURRISH;
He tells of a lady " complacently dying!"
'Tis thus that he hugs his political lying,
With words often wise—his whole life is a sample
Of all that is thoroughly base in example;
He shrewdly declines his opponents to meet,
In personal conflicts, *except in the street;*

---

with which it fortifies itself in all its positions, it would, perhaps, be still more wonderful if its influence were less felt. Some of its daily editorials and much of its correspondence are among the most masterly productions that ever graced our literature and language. We doubt not that its leading articles, if directed to those objects, would do as much to check fillibustering, border warfare, or at least border ruffianism and Know-Nothingism among us, as the ablest of our Presidential messages and of the speeches delivered in Congress. This may be unpalatable, but is it not true? The London *Times* has, since the commencement of our civil war, lost all its influence among the loyal citizens of the loyal States. Its prophecies were false, its positions untenable, its abuse of our Government unwarrantable, and its laudation of our enemies not unfrequently unjust and invidious.

* The vanes of a kite—"The vane is the thin membranous web of a feather on the side of the shaft."—PALEY.

For thither his satellites throng to support him,
With a chance, *ten to one,* that *no weapon shall hurt him;*
Or that he may fearlessly *shoot* from a *crowd*
Of ruffians, athirst for his enemies' blood;
But should *he* a *rival* or *murder* or *wound*—
His plea, "*self-defence,*" no indictment is found.
'Tis thus the arch-rioter plans to escape
The meshes of law by the tissue of tape;
A thing so effete and decrepit from vice—
No *man* would encounter, no *woman* entice;
Albeit, it is said, he has tools at his will,
To pander and riot, shoot, buffet, and kill.

His quacks are all Galens, his actors all Garricks,
His poets all Homers, his Harlequins Yoricks,
His Ethiop minstrels imported Tuaricks,
His trulls of the ballet excel Taglioni,
His songstresses—Malibran, Lind, and Alboni;
His chief violin, so much like Paganini,
Is worthy the muse of Mozart and Rossini—
Who backs him in *alt, double bass, pirouetting*
On key-notes of type, will scarce lose by his betting.
His lady contributors—Sapphos, Aspasias—
Are graceful and bright as our brightest acacias;
And be it admitted, he has the great merit
To foster in *them* a poetical spirit;—
A poet himself, both in thought and expression,
We owe him thus much in the way of concession.
His statesmen are far beyond Tully or Pitt,
The pillars of freedom, the lights of debate.
His fairs, exhibitions, renowned auctioneers,
Nor eyes have seen equalled, nor heard of men's ears.
In heroes and orators, gentlemen, look ye!
All ancients and moderns must yield to Kentucky!

Such, sirs, are his magical touches with dollars,
To change black to white in desert or in colors.
He now seems at rancorous feud with the Flaskoes—
Cousins-german in all diabolic *fiascos*.
Both wights are the veriest Barnums of type,
Both animals, too, of a synchronous stripe—
Or, birds if you will, of such beak and such feather
That all ornithologists class them together;
Yet, both of a trade, they can never agree
In aught, save in taking a bribe or a fee;
While one, if he could, would make ready for fight,
The other trusts more to a criminal writ;
Indeed, it appears from our criminal dockets,
That whips and ratans have, with gold, filled his pockets;
The other poor imbecile vastly prefers
To risk his own skin and set friends by the ears.
Sir Oracle, now of the Know-Nothing school,
A crutch for his wand, and his tripod a stool;
He always, for suitable victuals and wages,
The Know-Nothing doom of our Union presages.
Our President, this time, the *idol* of *one*,
The *other* regards as a *fox* or *raccoon;*—
"*Hic opere struit sublime theatrum,*
Et iste? quid refert? par nobile fratrum!"

Another there is, in a city where beans,
By some are much prized, as they rhyme with Orleens; *
But he of small beer or potatoes a type is,
Or aught thin and fragile as stem of a pipe is,
Or *twelfth of a musket-ball cut through the middle*—
To guess who he is, is not much of a riddle.

---

* "I like *beans*," said a prating little lawyer once to S. R.; "because," he added, "they rhyme with *Orleens*." "Query," said our friend Prosody. This corrupt pronunciation is not uncommon *even in the South*.

YOUNG AMERICA.

Grammarians that figure *synecdoche* call,
Which *all* for a *part*, or a *part* puts for *all*—
What a thing to resemble the pan of a head,
As postage stamp *thin* and as heavy as lead;
Round too, like a wafer, *diameter* same,
And eke the periphery—give it a name!
Good friend, if your rhyme be not much out of tune,
You will find it, I think, in the word Pic—y—u—ne.
He finding the Know-Nothing cause would not pay,
Abandoned his colors and scampered away;
A certain appendage behind him concealing—
'Twas all of the creature that had any feeling.

If Irish and German and French foreign labor
Abandon his city, how vain his endeavor
Its cycle to fill from the shape of a crescent! *
'Tis hoping old age will become adolescent.
One would think yellow fever, and drunkenness, and vice,
And *murder*, to *thin* the doomed place, would suffice,
Without native factions, to cause the expulsion
Of all those most likely to stop a convulsion
In commerce, and trade, and improvement, and *all*
The employments of life; nay, a ruinous fall,
To cities, and kingdoms, and empires, and states,
Whose wreck from sedition and tyranny dates;
When Pic. shall have paid for day's work a five-dollar
  Gold-piece to the hodman employed on his house,
It will add, or we err, a wee bit to his choler
    To think of the *insults*, the *oaths*, and the *vows*
He heaped and made use of in *Know-Nothing phrase*,
To *banish free labor, slave wages to raise.*
We, Yankees! to working, prefer being "*bosses!*"—
    In jobbing, contracting, lie mainly our skill:—

---

* New Orleans is called the *Crescent City*.

YOUNG AMERICA.

If as tradesmen we *fail*, we make up for our losses,
   With good *foreign craftsmen* to work out our will.
We often *Know Nothing* of what we engage in—
   Our foreigner *foreman* will look to our *text ;*
But, keen observation soon learns a page in
   Those rules which will always hold good till the next,
I mean the next scaffold, a rest to our feet is—
   We then look around at our altitude crowing—
Nor less at our skill to perfection fast growing !
This, all must admit, highly proper and meet is.

CANTO V.

Shows how certain Gentlemen would change their key-notes of Political turbulence if Emigration were to set in to some other quarter of the Globe. This no trivial matter. What the Country would lose. Political enemies. True Sons of Freedom contrasted with audacious Swaggerers and Preteuders to Independence. The conduct of the latter in Foreign Countries. How they deport themselves in the presence of European Sovereigns. Queen Victoria, Louis Philippe, Louis Napoleon, Oily Gammon, Influence of the Press, Sam Slick, and the Great Republic. Boundary lines Men. Diplomatic Peddlers. Harney and Douglas. North and South. Fillibusters. Walker and his Men. Paulding. Parallel Cases. Wolf. Senator Pierce. Cuba, Nicaragua, Indian Territories. Annuities. Houston. Benton. Carving out States and Territories. Indian Tribes. Our mammoth Commonwealth and John Bull.

I.

Ye, who in numbers so delight !
   Arithmeticians, Algebraists !
Of every creed and dogma hight,
   From Millerites to Monotheists,
Subtract, divide, and multiply,
   Add and reduce by static table,
Then frankly tell the reason why
   To calculate you are not able,
The boundless gain from immigration,
But, most of *all*, to this great nation.

Suppose *Know-Nothings* keep away
   One hundred thousand strangers yearly;
Supposing each of those to lay
Up for his wants, ten guineas nearly,
Or louis, pistoles, ducats, pounds,
   That he may not be, on first landing,
Reduced to want, lest he his "*standing*"
Should lose; or, e'er he makes his rounds,
To seek some suitable employment—
   Some fifty dollars, told in guineas,
Is no large sum to foreign ears,
   Who brings much less, or counts in pennies,
Sans hope of work or health's enjoyment,
   May often have to sup on tears!
Admit the aggregate amount,
Is not a sum of small account
In certain business speculations,
It swells beyond one's expectations;
   Count of their industry, the worth,
The houses built, the lands reclaimed,
   The vessels manned, the troops recruited,
   The mountains levelled, trees uprooted,
The knowledge spread, the statutes framed;
From East to West, from South to North,
The shops, the stores, the mines supplied,
On roads, canals, the labor plied,
   The value of domestic servants,
In hewing wood and drawing water;
Nay, call not this a trivial matter,
   Or scarcely worthy your observance.
The man who, with a wall of fire,
   Would stay the tide of emigration,
May live to witness his desire;
   By means of native legislation.

II.

Not many bite the hand that feeds them,
Not many kiss the hand that bleeds them,
Not many praise the tongue that slanders,
Not many pay the print that panders
To the worst passions of their foes,
The origin of countless woes—
Not many *lick* the barb that *tears* them,
Not many *press* the *brand* that *sears them*,
Not many hate a kindly neighbor,
Or think that *threats* of *knife* or *sabre*
    In pay for *work* or pay for *votes*,
Which they, as *freemen freely render*,
Should be esteemed a legal tender;
    Like other promissory notes,
They're somewhat of a *doubtful* gender!

III.

True sons of freedom act not thus,
Like Bushman, Boer, Kamtschatka-Russ;
One finds them gentle, courteous, gracious,
Not fiercely brutal, rude, audacious.
   *   *   *   *   *   *   *

IV.

Nor yet a second Oily Gammon,
Who worships God much less than Mammon;
Superior far to Samuel Slick—
    Eschewing slang in all his speeches—
He would not for the world pick
    One's pockets, yet he overreaches;
Makes it appear, at least he tries to,
In foreign parts, where'er he hies to,
That here our journals have no force,
That nothing follows, as of course,

Which they predict or wish to teach;
Exponents only of those views
Which they initiate or choose,
As most conducive to their profit,
And all the consequences of it.
"The people *act*, the journals *preach*"—
Peripatetic lions thus
Most infamously slander us;
Where'er their semi-regal faces
Shine, 'tis to squint at certain places.
If journals once the truth discover,
As touching every such rover,
'Tis ten to one they will defeat them,
Or teach some vulgar chuff to beat them
At all the Punchinello dodgings
Of our political dislodgings.
'Tis to the teachings of the Press
That all our public men confess,
They owe the fame of their success—
Be it or on the bench or stage,
Or in commercial patronage;
Or at the hustings or the bar,
Or 'Change, or other thoroughfare;
Or in the councils of the State,
Or in congressional debate,
Or in the pulpit or convention,
Met for polemical contention:
Sometimes political, alas!
Where *resolutions fail to pass*
Of thanks to God for putting down
Pro-slavery rebellion;
Or in the literary page
Asserting freedom's heritage,
Or in the diplomatic skill
Of some great statesman calm and still,

Who moulds whole nations to his will;
Or in the battle's hideous roar,
And echoing peals from shore to shore,
Or on the land or on the sea
Proclaiming rout or victory;
Or in the soarings of the muse,
While rapt in ecstasy she views
That which in poesy and art
Inspires and elevates the heart.
    Who doubts the press or will not own
As a great power in a realm,
To aid the chief who holds the helm;
To keep and guide the mighty ship,
Or in or out the harbor slip;
Or through the billows of the ocean
Of some fierce popular commotion,
    Is *but the more a fool or clown.*

v.

There is, who of the type *Sam Slick*,
At no dishonesty would stick;
Given to diplomatic peddling,
And parliamentary intermeddling;
His *idol* is a boundary line,
Or of St. Lawrence or East Maine;
Or through St. Juan, near Saltillo,
Or 'tween Omoa and Truxillo,
Or Nootka Sound and Rio Gila,
Or Caiman Lake, in Coahuila,
Mosquito Shore and Consiguina,
Or other fitting place between-a!
Glorious land, in our opinion,
For propagating slave dominion.

VI.

Van Couver's Island on the North,
And Costa Rica on the South,
  Should also be *embraced*, the *former*
Throughout the whole of its extent,
On this our Northern continent
(We mean, of course, pray mark it *well*,
Of *Latitude* the parallel)—
  Would both the Canadas take in,
Beside the Island of St. Juan—
Meet subject for some future Duan—
As late of mingled wrath and blarney,
Between the Douglas and the Harney!
And Anti-Costi, and so forth,
All to the Great West River North;*
    The *latter*—those who like a warmer—
    Climate would suit through Darien ·
Thus giving to us Carthagena,
And the sweet City of Cumana,
And all the trade of Oronoco:
Hides, coffee, indigo, and cocoa,
And all our VERY BEST TOBACCO!
No better market on the earth
For slaves of home and foreign birth;
Nor where from Africa transported,
They could so safely be escorted.

VII.

From ten degrees to fifty-five,
Thus owning, we are bound to thrive.
Quoth Sam: Nay, we should take the whole,
Both North and South, to either pole.

---

* The Northwest River, passing through the southern part of Labrador, falls into the Straits of Bellisle.

This is the programme of our Walker,
And he is something more than talker;
Not like our Quitmans, Fabens, Borlands,
Though they, too, greatly covet more lands;
But *he*, by hook or crook, will have them,
Or with men's skeletons will pave them.
Nolus volus! is the word with him,*
No puling fillibusters herd with him;
Sighing for money and for arms,
They first mark out their future farms;
Then rob and murder, scouting fears,
Like all determined Buccaneers,
Whose trust is chiefly in their triggers,
To find plantations full of niggers.
Quoth B.: Dear sir, but is it fair,
To hang John Brown and Walker spare?
They go, by Jove, the entire hog, sir!
Though all should hang for it, like dogs, sir!
They beat not round and round, but push
Right to the middle of the bush;
But if the bush should prove too hot,
A burning bush or blazing moat,
"They yield," cried C., "or compromise,
To brood o'er new atrocities!"
'Twas thus of late, in Nicaragua,
The selfsame felon sought to plague you a-
Gain, divine and human laws
He scorns, in both detecting flaws;
He breaks parole, renews aggression,
And labors hard to take possession
Of States which once had cast him forth,
To seek a refuge farther North.
'Tis true, with unsurpassed ill luck,
His expedition ends in smoke,

---

* "*Nolus volus.*" These words were called "General Taylor's Latin."

YOUNG AMERICA.

A *fumum ex fulgore* issue,
Befitting plots of such a tissue.
Thy fulgor, Paulding! is *ex fumo*,
A pyramid of *light* to loom o-
'Er ages yet unborn, when thou
Shalt, like thy sire, increasing grow
In fame *unisonant* with *duty*,
Memnonian chords! irradiate beauty!*
Yet Paulding little more than censure
Receives for checking this adventure.

VIII.

If when a wolf a neighbor's fold
Invades, shall we be gravely told
We must composedly look on,
To see them slaughtered, every one,
Nor should unto the rescue fly,
    To punish violence and wrongs,
Usurping the authority
    Of him to whom the fold belongs?
Now Walker, as a wolf, invades
With bands of lawless renegades—
    Rapacious, thievish, ravenous—
A neighboring state at peace with us,
Its herds and flocks to kill and fleece;
And tho' oft cautioned, will not cease
To bring about a revolution
Against our laws and constitution—
With men and means provided *here!*
In short, *declared* a *Buccaneer.*

---

* The Statue of Memnon (*Memnonis saxea effigies*) near Thebes, in Egypt, was said to give forth amelodious sound every day at sunrise.—TACITUS, *Annals,* ii., 61.

    Dimidio magicæ ubi Memnone chordæ
  Atque vetus Thebe centum jacet obruta portis.
                           JUVENAL.

Shall we ? or shall we not, though landed,
And with his ruffian rabble banded—
Pray mark, too, on a sandy point,
Where any honest neighbor, joint
Possession would accord another,
That came to succor as a brother—
See him destroy a friendly state;
Yet deem it proper to await
Till its inhabitants, like sheep,
Within a tiger's fatal sweep,
Behold themselves and rulers slain,
Nor yet have reason to complain
That we have suffered them to be
The victims of his tyranny ;
Or, of *our cruel apathy !*
All this, because the law of nations,
By most gratuitous illations,
Requires, *some think*, that any power,
Or *equal* or *superior*,
Should rather see another die,
Than violate neutrality !*

---

* An abstract in the *National Intelligencer*, of a speech delivered in Congress by Mr. Pearce, of Maryland, on the 28th of January, 1858, fell under the observation of S. R. soon after he had written the above rhymes. The speech referred to, reflects equal honor upon the head and heart of the distinguished Senator. Walker, he said, if only guilty of a misdemeanor against the municipal law of our own country, was, in every sense of the term, a freebooter and a pirate against the sovereign territorial rights of Nicaragua. In the light of general principles (which Mr. P. had most ably illustrated), he went on to say that the quality of Commodore Paulding's conduct, in compassing the arrest of Walker, could be clearly apprehended. Punta Arenas, where that arrest took place, might almost be regarded as derelict territory. Certain it was, that Nicaragua had no actual or potential jurisdiction over it. If not ousted by Costa Rica, she was, at least, ousted by Walker, when he landed and took possession of the locality in question. Nicaragua being thus powerless, at this point, it was no assumption on the part of Commodore Paulding, to suppose her sovereignty waived, in behalf of those

Ah, me, how feeble are our aids
To border nations in these raids!
But let the evil touch our own,
As in the case of old John Brown,
How quick, how furious is our vengeance,
How little is our condescendence!
Suppose adventurers from Cuba
Proclaimed, as free, the sons of Juba
In our Slave States; and driven thence,
Again renewed their insolence,
With or without consent of Spain—
Would any Southern man complain,
That we pursued them to Cardenas,
Or, if you will, to Punt Arenas,
And, or in *port* or *bare terrene*, ass-
Ailed and captured, whipt and banged them;
Or from our yard-arms strung and hanged them,
Without consulting Nicaragua,
Or Spain, or *caring* 'neath *what flag* we, a-
Land* or sea, or fought, or found them,
Or how we pommelled, killed, or drowned them!
No, no! those orators who now
Our Paulding's conduct disallow,
Would only then think Paulding right,
When boldly entered into fight;

who landed as her friends and allies. In the present case, Nicaragua, through her recognized minister, had solicited an interference, at this very point, for the prevention of Walker's descent.

Again, if any error had been committed by Com. P., it was not "a grave one," but was just such conduct as might have been expected from a bluff and honest sailor, anxious to do his duty and to protect the honor of his country. He, Mr. P., desired to see the Government vigilant, but just and courteous in its foreign intercourse, and he would have it magnanimous towards feeble powers. Especially did he expect it to crush, with a broad and heavy hand, the turbulent spirits who rebel against the restraints of municipal and international law.

* Aland—the word is used *adverbially.*

YOUNG AMERICA.

Would, to a man, the foremost be
To rail at such neutrality
As condign punishment presents,
To thieves, in action or intents.
The thieves who seek to make *them* martyrs,
Will find they've caught a nest of *Tartars*.
Alas! some strange delusion spreads
Cimmerian darkness o'er their heads,
Quoth B., they will not see a sin
Beneath a fillibuster's skin!
The South and Walker, slaves and felons,
And piccaroons with vulture talons,
Plunder and havoc lands laid waste—
Rape, murder, incest, shrines defaced,
Are but mere matters of opinion,
To those who *lust* for *slave dominion!*

All Southern States, rejoined Sam, must be ours, sir!
For we to control them, alone, have the power, sir!
To keep our good people from constant vexation,
We need the *prestige* of our loved annexation—
Nor can we maintain all our world-wide renown,
Except we thus constantly add to our own
Other lands: we as yet rank but fifth in accessions—
Brazilian, Chinese, British, Russian possessions*

---

* Our latest authorities furnish the following table, in square miles, of the countries referred to:—

Russian Possessions in square miles	7,540,402
Chinese Empire	5,000,000
British "	4,131,333
Brazil	3,956,800
United States	3,384,865

See "*Harper's Gazetteer*" and "*Colton's Atlas.*"

"*One to ten!*
Lean, raw-boned rascals, who would n'er suppose
They had such courage and audacity?"
Shakspeare, HEN. VI., Act 1st, Scene 1st.

Are larger than ours—but this ought not to be,
We must be ascendant by land and by sea:
'Tis true *many* nations in *numbers* surpass us,
But that is no standard by which men should class us—
Compare *us* with *others* in *war*, and so *forth*,
Our *one* counts for *ten* in *importance* and *worth!*
Besides, with a progress wholly unmatched, sir,
We alone may count chickens before they are hatched, sir!
Nor—such are our wisdom, our laws, and our mines.
Like Rome, be in terror of " falls or declines"—
Men not to be hanged or beheaded and quartered,
Should at least, replied B., have their state somewhat altered;
We must for our felons, so badly divided,
Have some penal colonies duly provided—
We view such possessions as national salves,
For States and for Empires, the best safety-valves;
Occasions arise, too, when corporate scape-goats
Are better preservers than canister-grape moats;
The Mormons, we think, may serve well for a sample,
Of all we need cite in the way of example;
Bodies politic, abscesses need for their tumors,
To rid them of some of their pestilent humors,
So, gases and vapors need pipes of escape,
Like those which the British possess at the Cape—
A word to the wise will convey our full meaning,
Tho' fools may not find it through volumes of scanning.

Those preachers we always least highly revere
Who tell us 'tis proper to *hope* and to *fear*—
That if we own slaves, it is not a good sign,
But a presage and proof of our speedy decline;
But those we esteem far above all the rest
Who tell us we are of all nations most bless'd!
The greatest, the happiest, wisest, and best!

And should, notwithstanding some national blotches,
Have faith in our cannons, our laws, and cartouches.

Thus he. Quoth Sam: Send Walker *north* of us,
Some great events will issue forth of us,
Thus verifying what was said
By some great poet long since *dead ;*
Matters it if his name was Tim,
Or Bill or Joel, Jack or Jim?
" No pent-up corner cramps our powers,
But the whole continent is ours!"*
We want no geographic scraps, sir,
We must have continental maps, sir:
This is our *motto :* " 'tis our *right,* sir,
Our *destiny,* and we *must fight,* sir!"
Have it we must, or I, by George, sir,
Will send my sword unto the forge, sir!
To be converted to a plough-share,
So may my country be my voucher!!

To balance well our slave and free States,
We ought to have a dozen sea States
On the Pacific—and, *inland*
A dozen more should take their stand;
Tracts, too, must farther *west* be found, sir,
To serve for Indian hunting-ground, sir!
Or else must fitting men instruct them,
And into civil ways conduct them;
They must have territorial laws, sir,
And no mistake—such is, or was, sir,
Our first intention when we gave them
Those lands which now so much deprave them,

---

* This very foolish boast—false when it was uttered, and still false—has, nevertheless, immortalized a sorry poet. Such, alas! are too often the stepping-stones to fame.

Or which they once, as more light-headed
Than we, for special objects ceded
To us: their murders,* feuds, and strife,
Their utter recklessness of life,
Their drunkenness—a besetting vice—
Their brutal, savage prejudice
Against the white man—these suffice,
Or should suffice to caution us
Against continual abuse.

*　　　*　　　*　　　*　　　*

Of wrongs, or fancied wrongs—their creed
Is to repay a deed for deed,
An eye for eye, or tooth for tooth;
Nay, rather 'tis, in very sooth,
Their creed to take two eyes for one,
Or, for *one tooth* take *all* or *none!*

We know these people far too well,
To think 'twill ever much avail,
If we their friendship would secure, Sir,
To give them other laws than ours, Sir,
The Choctaws, Chickasaws,† and Creeks,

---

* An ex-chief of a certain tribe, whose son was lately assassinated, being advised to make his case known to the Governor (the present title of the national chief), replied, as he dropped the end of his rifle on the ground: "I know no *governor but this!*"

† In the Appendix (Part V., pp. 693–4) to Schoolcraft's excellent work on the "History, Condition, and Prospects of the Indian Tribes of the United States," there is, in a letter from one J. A. H., who calls himself a member of the Choctaw Nation, and writes, April 15th, 1855, a glowing (query, glozing!) account of the present prosperity of these people.

The statistics as to schools are not much exaggerated, save in describing them as second to none in the United States. This is a little too barefaced, even for the credulity of his Indian readers. He speaks of their laws as comparing favorably with those of many of the States. That may well be, as they are taken *verbatim et literatim* (with essential modifications) from the laws of a neighboring

As all our best experience speaks,
The Seminoles and Cherokees
Will never be true feodaries
Of ours, excepting in appearance,
Until they learn, by our forbearance,
To wait such processes of court
As with our civil laws comport:
Besides, our march is upward, onward;
Nor must we let them sink far downward,
But rather carry them along—
So weak men always yield to strong.
Our o'erland route sufficient pledge is
That now, at last, the entering wedge is
Fairly impacted to the heart
From which that life-blood is to start,
Which gives new vigor to the growth
Of every State and nation South—
Where—for the thing is fairly planned—
All white men who shall make a stand
Shall each his nigger have, and laud:
Ay, land enough, we pledge *our* word,

State. When he goes on to say that those laws are generally respected and obeyed, he states that which is the very reverse of truth. There is not a community on the globe, with any pretension whatever to Christianity and civilization, among whom law is so little regarded, and horrid murders so frequent. In fact, their present leading men see no other hope for them, nor *is* there, if they would be saved from utter extirpation—by internecine violence—than handing them over to the territorial jurisdiction of the United States.

As respects the fields of golden grain, the industry, the neat and comfortable dwellings, the shrill whistle of the steam-engine echoing, &c.—echo answers *where?*—where, but in the imagination of H.? There was, it is true, once upon a time, one steam-whistle in the place referred to, but it is gone like H. Finally, this man *is not*, never *was*, and assuredly never *will* be, a member of the Choctaw Nation. He was, for a short time, printer and editor of a little newspaper, which failed in his hands, and would have failed in the hands of a far *better man*.

To suit a nabob or a lord.
Indians, in short, must be subdued,
However turbulent or rude,
And law maintained and rights defended,
Far as our limits are extended.
All the annuities we pay them,
Alas! tend only to betray them
To trading sharks, who closely watch them,
And with vain baubles basely catch them,
As fish or birds are caught by hooks
With gudgeons baited, or with flukes:
Besides, they have no wish to toil,
Or cultivate a grateful soil—
So long as they expect a pension,
By statutory intervention,
Rather than make the least endeavor,
They hope and hope, and hope forever,
And hoping thus, they far prefer
To starve than labor half the year:
They also are in mines too rich,
Coal, marble, granite, tar, and pitch
In lead, in copper mines, in iron,
And other things which so environ
Or fill their lands, that we must be
The veriest ninnies not to see
It is our interest and our duty,
A soil of so much wealth and beauty,
So fit for pasture, agriculture,
And all those products which most nurture
Arts, commerce, sciences, to *own*,
As of our sinew and our bone;
Our railroads must to the Pacific
Pursue their course, with trains magnific,
And to our country most lucrific,
Within ourselves, thus made *Omnific*.

YOUNG AMERICA.

As in Nebraska and in Kansas
We've made our territorial plan pass,
So treat we every Indian nation,
With or without their approbation.
So shall we soon treat Arizona,
Where Samuel Houston would atone a-
New for all his past transgressions,
In fillibustering invasions,
And end his days in rural peace,
The Jason of a golden fleece!
Or, lord of the Mesilla Valley,
In vineyards rich as Elealé!
He, with our Benton, in creation
Of States, ranks foremost in our nation;
While one is sketching them on paper,
The other marks them with a scraper,
Or deftly cuts them, like a draper,
Or shears them as he shears his wool,
Or carves them as he carves a spool,
Or on his hickory a noll!
Or pares them as a piece of ginger,
Or twists as fillets round his finger!

Regarding treaties of alliance,
We well may bid the world defiance,
To show a nation such as ours, sir,
That has not more abused its power, sir.
These half-breed fellows are the worst
Among the tribes—a race accursed:
'Tis easier far to tame the savage,
Who roams at large, to kill and ravage,
Than (*save by bribes!*) insure subjection
From men so wanting in affection,
As are these treacherous demi-devils,
The cause of most our Indian evils!

We want all the lands of the Iroquois tribes, sir,
Or else, we must, very soon, tread on their kibes, sir;
The Senecas, Mohawks, Cayugas, Oneidas,
Wyandots, Shawnees, Tuscaroras, as wide as
The Chippewas, Ottowas, Weas, Miamies,
Wherever on Michigan waters their claim is,
The Delawares, Kickapoos, Ottoes, Peonies,
Sacs, Foxes, Piankeshaws, Crees, Menomōnies—
They dwell on Missouri, Platte River, the Kansas,
Not far from the powerful Sioux, whose advance, as
The newspapers tell us, extending far west,
For them and for us is alike for the best—
Must all be soon ceded as Free or as Slave States,
For so irrepressible conflicts will have States.
The giant Osages, the Quapaws and Poncas,
The Crows and the Mandans and Cheyennes, tho' once as
Distinguished in war as the best of their race,
To many beneath them are now giving place;
The Kichies and Caddoes, Apaches and Wacos,
Comanches and Wichits,* Pawnees and Andacos—
Their lands on the Llano, Red River, and Brazos
Are ours, as migration progressively draws us
And must, as some think, till the conflict be ended,
For slaves and their masters be chiefly intended.
In Oregon, too, we but name the Cayuses,
The Chatsops and Tillamooks, Umpquaws, Paloosas,
The Wascopans, Spokans, the Snakes and Mallallas,
Orilles, Okonnagans, Rogues,† and Walwallas,
Nez-Perces, Des Chutes, Sinhumānish, Klackamas—
Wheelapas, Vancouvers, Timwaters, Yahamas—
All, all must depart, or be wholly absorbed, sir,
And see all their titles completely usurped, sir!

---

* Wichitaws.
† Indians on Rogue River.

A mammoth Commonwealth like ours
Must dwarf all other human powers;
In Oregon, one fore-foot's planted,
For t'other, Canada is wanted;
The hinder two will need Brazil—
It suits them singularly well.
One heel, perhaps, may press Peru,
But what is that to me or you?
We care not to be thought Peruvians—
Content with being "border ruffians;"
The British, Greenlanders, and Russians
For head and horns will give possessions;
The body with the middle place
Will be contented, if there's space
Sufficient left to take repose,
Or for the rump, or for the nose;
The flanks may get a little wet,
And cause an inconvenient jet
On Florida or New Granada,
Mayhap ingulfing a llanada *
On either coast: the hip, on Hayti,
Would, in its *hollow, so conceit ye,*
Protect both Cuba and Jamaica.
Ye British! how we then might rake ye!
The tail will lash the angry water,
And fill both oceans with huge slaughter,
Submerging all the small-fry islands
With Porto Rico and some highlands,
If foreign powers forget Monroe,
And cruise with frigates to and fro,
Or tamper much with Mexico—
(For she is ours, but in abeyance,
Waiting the process of conveyance)!

---

* Llanada means in Spanish a wide tract of level ground—a plain.

Or lash the Caribbean Sea,
Down South, as far as Uruguay;
Or from the Northern Archipelago,
As far as Terra Della Fuego!
In short, dear sir, we'll give them h—l,
If they against our wish rebel!

John Bull, in Asia, works destruction
　　To native States—why not John Mammoth,
Who always "betters his instruction,"
　　Push from the land the priests of Ramoth?*

CANTO VI.

THE TRUE AMERICAN.

I.

A TRUE American is he
Who marks the bounds of liberty,
Whose head, and heart, and purse, and hand
Would aid th' oppressed in every land,
Not in a fruitless, vain crusade,
Or pageantry of masquerade;
Nor yet, in gasconading speeches,
Which in a fortress make no breaches;
Not threatening, as a fillibuster,
A host of valiant men to muster,
Altars and empires to o'erthrow,
And turn their joy to notes of woe:

---

* *Ramoth.*—"And Zedekiah, the son of Chenaanah, made him horns of iron: and he said, Thus saith the Lord, With *these shalt thou push the Syrians,* until thou have consumed them. And all the prophets prophesied so, saying, Go up to *Ramoth-Gilead* and prosper: for the Lord shall deliver it into the king's hand."— 1 Kings xxii. 11, 12.

But here at home, assist each neighbor
To profit by his honest labor;
The widow help, the orphan cherish,
Nor suffer any one to perish,
Whom Christian charity can save
From filling an untimely grave!
Who means and influence would expend
Free trade and commerce to extend,
Encourage foreign immigration,
As well as slave emancipation,
And African colonization,
And peace with every race and nation.
Diffuse religion, science, art,
The head enlighten, mend the heart;
Genius of every clime and creed
Assist and cheer in time of need;
Instructing in true courtesy
Barbarian, Scythian, bond and free.
A type of all that's great and good,
In virtue, learning, noble bearing,
He wears no mask, he needs no hood,
Brave, open, honest, ever daring.
To speak the truth, he dreads no jeers,
   No threats of violence and faction,
No mob or Lynch-law fury fears—
   In speech sincere and cool in action.
He feels no sense of degradation
In honoring worth in any station;
To equals courteous, yet, not hoping
To influence their choice by stooping
To craft or skill in pulling wires,
If he to power or place aspires;
Not thankless for a favor rendered,
He can, with grace, decline one tendered.
From platform calumny and wrath,

He flies, as from a viper's path;
Friendship not rash to *antedate*,
Yet *fixing, fixes, fast as fate;*
He keeps the promise he has made,
He hates caprice in man or maid;
His dress his station ever fitting,
The *"juste milieu"* in all things hitting.
We hail these qualities as real
In gallant Clay, our *beau-ideal.*
As certain stones will point where gold is,
As gold of character the mould is,
As fire, your drossy gold refining,
Proves what is *pure, so, in divining*
The human mind, there is a test
Infallible of what is best:
Our model character to scan,
We sketch a *true American,*
In dignity and elevation
A normal type for every nation;
And giving to the whole *physique*
An air half Roman and half Greek.
Such men were Everett and Irving,
So great, so good, and so deserving—
(Our martyred Lincoln ranks before,
Or Consul, King, or Emperor
Of Greece or Rome!); and such is Chase—
Reflecting lustre on our race;
Such is the lion-visaged Scott,
Such Seward and Sumner, without blot;
Grant, Sherman, Thomas, Farragut;
And more than such was Washington,
Unblamed, unrivalled, and alone!

CANTO VII.

Who are Americans in the strictest sense. All that we have and are, due to Europe. Paupers. Their support. Free labor compared with Slave labor. Worth of the former to this Country. Nothing to be feared from Roman Catholics. What is really to be feared. Religious Schisms. Dishonesty in our Markets exemplified. Scant fare at Restaurants. How rich criminals escape justice, while the friendless are punished. Want of discipline. Crittenden. Marshall. Fillmore.

I.

BEARS, bisons, wolves, and alligators,
And all such savage, brutal creatures,
Insects and reptiles, a whole host of,
We leave to Know-Nothings to boast of.
As *natives*: customs, rites, and manners,
Our commerce, trade, and agriculture,
Arts, armies, navies, owe their nurture
To European laws and banners;
All somewhat modified, no doubt,
By influences *within, without.*
Yet all we are, and all we have,
From our first statesman to the slave
Who cultivates our grain and cotton,
We owe to Europe, though forgotten
By men *unthankful* and unkind,
Wilfully ignorant and blind;
Who now, on strangers, would bestow
A frightful heritage of woe.

II.

Paupers, indeed, there are among us,
But do these paupers greatly wrong us?
Our immigrants pay vast expenses:
What man is there who, in his senses,
Denies that capitation fees,
From all who cross Atlantic seas,

And eke Pacific, be they yeomen,
Mechanics, laborers, children, women,
Two dollars each, go far to pay
For burials, physic, and would say
That those who in our country's service
Or die of wounds, are mad or nervous,
Should not, in sickness, be attended,
Or be in anywise befriended?
The cost of justice, we opine,
Is greatly aided by the fine
Imposed by judges in the State*
Where men offences perpetrate.

III.

Free labor is as *five* to *three*,
Compared with *working Slavery;*
A thousand dollars is the price,†
In fields of sugar-cane or rice,
At which a single slave is rated:
Now say that this is estimated
To be the value of the labor,
Of any Scotch or Irish neighbor,
Who, by his hands and sweat of brow,
May earn his bread with spade or plough;
And say one hundred thousand yearly
Of such day-laborers, or nearly,
Come to our coasts; one hundred millions—
We might go on to count in billions—

---

* The aggregate amount of pecuniary fines throughout the towns and cities of the United States, for crimes and misdemeanors, must be enormous. To one not conversant with police reports in New Orleans, their amount in that city alone seems absolutely incredible.

† This estimate of Adam Smith, in the "Wealth of Nations," differs little from the present market value of slaves.

Would be the constant annual gain
Which follows in the prosperous train
Of European emigration,
To swell the coffers of our nation.
The Asiatic we pass by,
It is not meet to amplify;
Albeit the California mines
Exact from China heavy fines.

IV.

Respecting Catholics, who fears
As much from them as from the jeers
Of countless sectaries and ranters,
And Atheistical dissenters,
Has yet to learn the a, b, c
Of Christian truth and polity.
In short, innumerable *isms*,
Politico-religious schisms,
The want of faith, the want of truth,
The want of modesty in youth,
The want of teachers who agree
In creeds—of parents, who foresee
What divisions these all will lead to;
What loose domestic ties are said to
Produce—at home, most sad misrule,
And worse, if possible, at school.
The want of honesty in trade,
Take for an instance one great curse,
Spread wide to pick the public purse,
Dead fowls with all their purtenance left,
Plus heads and legs for market heft;
And pinions and some feathers, too,
Are weighed in balances not true,
Their craws and paunches filled and crammed,

Nay, oft with grain and gravel rammed,
To cheat some honorable fool
Who buys through fear of ridicule,
And for his *offal pays as much*
As though sound flesh had filled each pouch.
In bills and fees, and false amounts,
Claimed on unwarranted accounts;
In spurious papers and bank-notes,
In buying and recording votes,
In oaths of office never kept,
To have our thoroughfares well swept;
Or, touching customs and excise,
Involving fiscal sacrifice.
In mixing deleterious drugs,
Wines, spirits, dyes, and hydragogues,
Fit work for scurvy thieves and rogues;
Nor less in shoddy goods we see
Our trafficking iniquity.
Whoso another instance wants,
May find it in our restaurants,
Where no one gets a *quantum suf.*
Of rations; nay, scarce half enough,
If with good appetite and health,
A worker for the commonwealth,
Yet he is forced for wafer slices
To pay unconscionable prices.
The sole exception Rubek knows
Is met with at Delmonico's,
Where citizens or aliens
Have all they wish and want, he weens,
And if they pay a little more
Than others ask; yet on that score
Not one complains, for all is right,
In price and quality and weight.
Alas! Delmonicoes are rare,

And more so still the liberal fare,
Which they provide for every guest
Who can upon their viands feast.

Ah! where shall now the suffering poor
Provide their food and shut the door
Against those wolves of gaunt disease
And want, which stalk abroad to seize
Those impotent to ward the blow
Of hunger, nakedness, or woe.
On such as triumph in the cheer
Of plenty, through the fruitful year,
Must strangers, orphans, widows call.
For He, the bounteous Lord of all,
Enjoins, commands, to bless and give,
And every child of want relieve.
On him who now in mercy sows,
And with a liberal hand bestows
His alms, or charitably lends,
And every human aid extends,
If change or chance should bring distress,
His soul in everlasting peace
Shall rest secure—his *shield* the *word*,
His *rock* the *promise of the Lord*.

Again must we our steps retrace,
With due regard to time and space.
The want of honesty in trade,
Of principle, in every grade;
The want of due subordination
To those who *rule*, in every station,
From those who *serve;* the daily life
Of license running into strife;
The want of filial love and fear,
To every true believer dear.

It is commanded in the Word
Of God, that "children in the Lord"
Obey their parents; yet we see
The precept, as in mockery,
Read backward thus: "Ye parents must
Obey your children, as is just!"
Pray is not such too oft the case
In this our selfish age of brass?
The mother is the daughter's drudge,
The son the sire's, and if a judge
Elected by the people's voice
Holds law and guilt in equipoise,
And feels disposed to visit sin
With salutary discipline,
The tenure of his seat in court
Must needs be onerous and short.
For all wrong-doers hate a man
Who dares their evil deeds condemn;
And having power, possess the will,
His place with supple tools to fill.

In thievish banking, now so rife,
We see the issue of the strife
'Tween principle and love of gain,
And other vices which obtain.
Our shortest catechisms teach
On these points all we fain would preach
Touching our duty towards our God—
What we must do and what avoid;
Our duty also towards our neighbor,
And towards ourselves—that we should labor
To get our living in some state
Which conscience deems legitimate;
Nor with our hands or pick or steal,
Or offer violence or kill;

Nor with our tongues or lie or slander,
Or to a brother's lapses pander.
But thieves are far too dignified,
With such plain teaching to be plied;
Our heartless Ketchums cannot see
The depth of their depravity.
'Tis true we have no lack of schools,
Imparting knowledge unto fools;
Yet want of pure religious training,
In thought and word and action reigning,
Among our youth, explains in all things
The dread abuses which befall things.
If to the masses they extend,
They must in general ruin end.
O Ketchum! Ketchum! now behold
The folly of your lust of gold;
The root of pride and every evil
Within the empire of the Devil!
The man who though by hunger led
Abstracts a loaf or two of bread,
Or poor and hapless orphan boy,
While vainly seeking some employ,
Who steals a watch or ring or chain,
Or say a golden-headed cane—
Is sent to expiate his crime
" For time and times, and half a time,"
Within the precincts of some jail,
Where such as he can never fail
To add to their iniquities
New lessons in the arts of vice.
But if one steal a hundred thousand
In bills and checks, and owns a house, and
Has land, possessions still in store,
Or still abounds in golden ore,
'Tis ten to one that he escape

By skilful management of tape,
By bribes that is, and by chicane
Of court tribunals, and their train
Of jurors, witnesses, and lawyers,
Hydraulic jacks for rich employers!
How oft do men with murder red,
Who at elections have been made
The tools of noted demagogues,
Or other over-reaching rogues,
Been known the gallows to elude
By means of such a brotherhood!
How oft in cases of divorce,
If those most guilty show most force
In friends or money, does success
Their undermining efforts bless.
Ah! *no : not bless, for what they sow*
In sin, they needs must reap in woe.
Enough thus said—par-parenthese,
We to our text return apace.

v.

Say! Fillmore, Crittenden, and Marshall,
Pike, Prentice, * * * say how far shall
The bounds of naturalization
Extend in your codification?
Defining rights, if rights you give
To men as worthy to receive
Those rights as *you* have proved to be,
In your broad views of liberty?
They understand our Constitutions,
And all our country's institutions;
Why should they not, if blest at all
With understandings such as fall

YOUNG AMERICA.

To most men's lot, in shorter time
Than that which comes to *half a dime*
Of *years ?* Their duty and their oath,
And solemn promises of both;
They know as well as *you* or *I*,
Who find in them no mystery.
If all may read and understand them,
Why *unintelligible brand* them?
Pray listen to an exile's song—
To you of right it doth belong;
In you, and such as you, *ambition*
May drag our country to *perdition ;*
Of reins executive, the power,
If you possess, in evil hour,
The day which ends our country's glory
Is come. Our *song contains a story.*

CANTO VIII.

The Emigrant's Song. Wandering Jew. Uzzah. Folly of rejecting Foreigners. Sevastopol. European dynasties. Our Constitution like the Ark upon the Flood, finally resting upon an Ararat of peace, and sending forth its olive-branch to all the nations of the earth.

EMIGRANT'S SONG.

I.

BACK, back to the land of your birth and your sires,
　Ye Emigrants, hasten! Columbia no more
Your skill, or your valor, or labor requires—
　She spurns you, as outcasts, away from her shore.
Descended from fathers who, strangers, like you,
　Sought safety and homes in these lands of the West;
Like so many Pharaohs, our Natives renew,
　While boasting of freedom, a religious test.

70

II.

In numbers now strong, and in riches increased,
   They need not your aid foreign foemen to fight,
Or fancy they need not; your valor has ceased
   To be prized as of yore in these days of their might.
Why crossed ye the ocean to peril your lives,
   In sickness and toil, want, and travail and woe?
Where many must perish, like bees in a hive,
   While Natives grow great by the sweat of their brow.

III.

From Liberty's birth-place—the home of the brave—
   As doves to their windows, so fly ye towards home,
Where freedom, less talked of, beholds not a slave,
   And all may, in concert, sing slavery's doom.
Like Jews to their Zion, then hasten ye East,
   To mingle your dust with the dust of your sires;
Sweet freedom, her altars thrown down in the West,
   May chance in the East to rekindle her fires.

IV.

Farewell to the relics of those that are sped,
   To whiten, like snow-spots, our Golgotha plains;
The tears they have wept and the blood they have shed,
   In vapors arising, descending in rains,
Proclaim with shrill plaints, in the hurricane's blast
   (As a dirge from the grave), that their friends are denied
Those blessings of freedom, for which, to the last,
   They had striven and struggled, and conquered and died.
Then back to the land of your birth and your sires,
   Ye Emigrants, hasten! Columbia no more
Your skill, or your valor, or labor requires—
   She spurns you, as outcasts, away from her shore. *

---

* The Emigrant's Song was written during the excitement occasioned by the

V.

Who rudely shakes or dares divide
   Our freedom's ark and sacred home,
Should die the death that Uzzah died,
   Or like that Jewish wanderer roam,
Who feels a never-dying death—
   Despised, estranged, forlorn;
And, in his every latest breath,
   Laments that he was born.

VI.

Dash not away, on futile grounds,
The ladder on whose faithful rounds
   Thou mounted'st far on high;
Thou may'st again its aid require,
In reaching summits which aspire
   To touch the starry sky.
Some battles may again be fought,
And victory be dearly bought,
And glory lost, or nobly won,
And *fame* more *durable* than *stone!*

VII.

With all thy bastions, gabions, towers,
Backed by the mightiest of powers,
   Thy gallant garrison, despite
Thy valor unsurpassed in fight,
And all thy scientific light—
   For of the cities nigh and far,

Louisville riots, and by no means expresses the present feelings and wishes of the writer, as respects a return to the Old Country. He has not failed, in other publications, to reprobate the conduct of the New York Irish rioters, as the tools of the Copperhead Peace-men.

None scarcely could with thee compare
In every art of war—
Yet thou, Sevastopol! at length,
   All citadels to warn,
Assaulted by superior strength,
   Hast greatly, grandly fall'n!
Thy fall the glorious epoch whence
We date thy chief magnificence,
   Thy diadem of thorn!
The places which retain in trust
   The armor thou hast worn,
Thy heroes' bones, where now, in dust,
   Thine honored trophies lie,
Shall ever, ever, noble town!
Be first in glory and renown,
   In war's sad history!

VIII.

Should Europe's thrones, with hostile bands,
Invade our peaceful, happy lands,
May we, in closest bonds allied,
Have always, fighting by our side,
Whate'er their forms or creed,
Where'er they first drew vital breath,
Or on the Shannon or the Tweed,
The Thames, the Vistula, the Seine,
The Po, the Danube, or the Rhine,
Good men and gallant men and free—
Not bastard sons of liberty,
But skilled in every martial deed,
   And daring unto death!

IX.

Borne like the ark upon the flood,
Through foaming billows streaked with blood,

Beneath a rainbow light,
Ah, may our Constitution float
Thro' winds and waves, and mark the spot
 (If we our banners raise in fight)
Round which the angry breakers beat,
In safety, as round Ararat;
And thence, with greeting, send its wand
Of joy and peace to every land.

YOUNG AMERICA.

TO THE MEMORY
OF
EDMUND BURKE,
WHO
DIED, MANY YEARS AGO,
AT
PETERSBURG, VIRGINIA.

"*Semper honos, nomenque tuum, laudesque manebunt.*"
Non ingenio quæsitum nomen ab ævo.
Excidet ; ingenio stat sine morte decus.

PREFACE.

THE prose works on Slavery which have lately issued from the press seem, with very few exceptions, to have perished at their birth. The reason probably is, that they were regarded by the public as mere essays upon a topic which, from constant discussion, like that of our great July celebration, presents nothing new to the reader or hearer.

And why, it may be asked, should these metrical effusions, by an author without *prestige*, and with small pretensions, comparatively, to an extensive acquaintance with literature—au author without friends, influence, commanding talents, or established local habitation—in short, one inevitably and hopelessly obscure—why or how should a work on Slavery, emanating from such a source, and compounded (as the reader of advertising columns will naturally—how erroneously soever—imagine it needs must be) of the commonplace views of Abolitionists, the hackneyed *diatribes* of their orators and scribes, be fated to any other than a sudden and unheeded extinction?

The Author grounds his hope of a different, nay, opposite result, upon the freshness, the truthfulness, the painfully interesting nature of the scenes he has ventured to describe, as well as upon the variety and novelty of his *manner of description*, as shown in his varied iambics.

Another ground of hope entertained by the Author, of a popular appreciation of these pages (as observed in his Preface to some poems, already published, on the same subject), is, that they address themselves successively—and may he trust, not unsuccessfully,—to the strongest sympathies of our nature; that they touch, in their nearest and dearest interests, all orders and degrees of human beings, all religious denominations and parties, all trades, professions, and occupations of life. Our octosyllabics have, in a word, what is so attractive to the millions—a tale or tales in them—that sort of human interest frequently wanting in more aspiring productions.

Of some of the scenes exhibited in the text and illustrations, the writer was an eye and ear witness; others were matters of daily conversation among his neighbors at the times and places when and where they had occurred. Even those which he has draped with such humor and satire as came at his bidding, are all substantially true.

PREFACE.

For the scenes in a Virginia tavern and court-house, he is, perhaps, more than editorially responsible; having retouched, amplified, and, in some instances, modernized them, so to speak, by interpolations of the text of a dear deceased friend and relative. They will, doubtless, be regarded by many as caricature *tableaux* of men and things as they existed some forty years ago in the Old Dominion. He unhesitatingly indorses them, and doubts not they will be recognized by others, as true and vivid pictures of those days, and of days somewhat later in its history.

The lines upon Legree, and those upon the Georgian, Cato D—le, and others, have tripped into their places so naturally, and with so very little effort to the writer, that he can scarcely persuade himself they cost him, in conception or construction, a moment's hesitation; or, that where any thing of dialogue occurs, they were not the *ipsissima verba* of the speakers. If poor Cato, and other *dramatis personæ* mentioned, had not expressed themselves in verse, they assuredly have said something so like what is here set down for them, that the writer is scarcely conscious of a variation from a single syllable ascribed to them. But of these things the reader will judge for himself.

Defects, anomalies, redundancies, mannerisms, pedantry, shortcomings, and overdoings of all kinds and degrees, will be, according to the temper in which it is read, urged against our homely little volume.

The occasional succession of rhymes in four consecutive lines, and the recurrence of the same or similar rhythmical sounds and terminations, at shorter intervals than seem warranted by the practice of certain eminent writers, nor less so, perhaps, the variety of metrical construction in one continuous composition—sanctioned though such variety be, especially in satire, by the examples of Boileau, Racine, the sweetest of our own English poets, and, passing over the satires of Ennius, Pacuvius, Licinius, in iambic, trochaic, hexameter verses* by one †who was emphatically *puri sermonis amator*—will be brought forward as evidence of unskillfulness, carelessness, ignorance, or want of power. But, all these objections notwithstanding, the Author finds, or thinks he finds, in the exercise of his own simple judgment, as good reasons for retaining his numbers as they now stand, as others can find for retrenching, recasting, or altogether suppressing them.

He has imitated no one—has borrowed from no one—save in those few instances in which imitation or quotation is acknowledged. The plan of his work is his own. It is all that he designed it to be. What in this little book many may, from a cursory view, regard as *disjecta membra*, will be found, upon closer examination, not wanting in the unities of dramatic action (unless when such unities should be properly disregarded), but "fitly joined together and compacted," ac-

---

* See Dacier's Preface to the Satires of Horace.   † Julius Cæsar.

PREFACE.

cording to the measure of a work of design—and that design or unity of object, *the utter abolition of negro slavery.* If he has, in a manner agreeable to his readers and just to himself, given utterance to important truths; if he has endeavored to pass "from gay to grave, from lively to serene," he is contented to leave to those of more distinguished reputation a brighter and less perishable garland.

In writing under a disguised signature, for reasons satisfactory to himself, Sennoia Rubek has only done what other and better writers have done before him. He wishes to preserve his *incognito* always, or, at least, until he gives to his readers—if he ever does—a production more worthy their perusal than the unadorned rhymes of these narratives.

For his Preface, Introduction, and Notes, our Author has no better apology to offer than that, such as they are, they will, probably, be as acceptable to his readers as any other portion of his work.

The advantage or expediency of at all discussing Slavery, in the present state, or in any state of excitement upon that subject, is the cardinal point of judgment in the matter of these poems. If Slavery be of God, as Mr. Bledsoe and others contend it is, we cannot abolish it. If it be not of God, it will come to nought.

We believe we have as good a right to discuss it as Mr. Bledsoe, Mr. Harper, Mr. Hammond, Professor Dew, Dr. Seabury, Dr. Raphael, Mr. Van Dyke, Bishop Hopkins, or any one else. Why not? The wisest and best men, and many of whom the world was not worthy, are to a man on our side, and we are perfectly willing to stand or fall with them. Possibly also we possess another right which certain gentlemen may feel more disposed to call in question—*the use of satire in our verses.*

Carmine mordaci populi depingere mores. It is not unlikely we may, with others, be accused of carrying our satire too far.

"*Sunt quibus in satira videar nimis acer, et ultra,
  Legem tendere opus.*"

The principle of saying nothing but good of the dead, would, if urged to its utmost extent leave us in utter ignorance of the history of mankind.

Many of the personal allusions found in these pages, and, whether direct or indirect, doubtless unpalatable to some of those for whom they are intended, as well as to their abettors and friends, relate to things of moment in the chronicles of our day. For these and certain other personalities, the advocates of Slavery have no one to blame but themselves. They have challenged public opinion, and must abide by its result.

Among planters and slave-owners there are many—there is one in particular—to the forfeiture of whose friendship by the present exposition, the Author looks forward with unmitigated pain.

PREFACE.

But enough; there never was a reform, religious or political, without a sundering of those ties which are nearest and dearest to the heart. If the Author has found, even in his own family, for years, the most vehement and persevering opposition to his anti-slavery principles and acts, and especially to the publication of these metrical prolusions, can he ever be surprised by an outcry from abroad?

The stanzas addressed to Her Majesty Queen Victoria, in a former publication, as well as the others In Memoriam, and those to the Emperors, were somewhat hurriedly introduced after all the other poems had been completed.

The first volume contains, besides our Spenserian stanzas, two cantos on the Brooks and Sumner affair, as growing out of the question of Slavery.

It is useless to speculate upon the popular reception of these satires, or their effects upon the friends of Mr. Brooks. Suffice it to say, that none of these pieces should ever see the light, were it not for the recommendation by the Governor of South Carolina of the re-establishment by law of the African slave-trade; the strenuous advocacy of that measure by many of the delegates to certain Southern conventions (though recently disavowed), and the laudation of the conduct of Brooks by certain writers and orators of the pro-slavery party.

The contemplated Index Expurgatorius of Southern school men, and the establishment, or intended establishment, of the so-called University of the South for the education of the sons of slaveholders, will account for the Song of the Students, and the *jeux d'esprits* addressed in the first volume to the Bishops and certain other ecclesiastics of the Slave States. The lines addressed to Mr. Pike, Mrs. Grundy, Mrs. Partington, and some prominent British and American statesmen, will speak for themselves, as will also the family pictures in the ballad stories of Little Fanny and Mary. Scenes in Congress and the Pro-Slavery Bishop would scarcely be out of place in any part of our works.

To the charges of disorganization, disunion, treason, perfidiousness, inordinate vanity, love of notoriety, &c., being the old stereotyped dodges against all who oppose slavery, we are not solicitous to reply. We believe, and have always believed, that those are the only true friends of our Union who advocate abolition, immediate or gradual, with the proviso of a suitable compensation to loyal slave-owners, and who urge upon the consideration of the national executive au earnest and vigorous co-operation in the suppression of the African slave-trade.

It is only in the estimate of such men as Governor Alston, of South Carolina, and the rebels now in arms against our Government, that we are not as good patriots as those greatest missionaries the world ever saw, viz.. piratical kidnappers, and the chivalrous consignees of their living human cargoes. It is only in the estimate of such men we are not as patriotic as those mild-spoken celebrities, who bring to the land of the free and the home of the brave hundreds upon hundreds and thousands upon thousands of our fellow-beings, forced to sit, or

PREFACE.

lie down spoon-ways, in holds and under hatches of corsair skippers, covered with vermin, inhaling putridity, steeped in filthiness, and, like our Union prisoners at the South, reduced to two-thirds of their number by starvation and disease. And why all this? To gratify the rapacity of slavers—the pride, cupidity, and ambition of a hard-hearted, insolent, and intolerant oligarchy.

But there must be no agitation of the question of Slavery—of course not; or, the discussion must be (Hibernice!) all on one side. These one-sided gentry are never aggressors, but peaceable, gentle, and easy to be entreated, as the records of Congress prove. Simms, Bledsoe, Hammond, and others may prose; Carolina Governors issue pronunciamientos; Virginia Governors, with more of ambition for the Presidency than zeal for the patriarchal institution, transgress the *ne quid nimis* by fuss and fustian; conventions pass resolutions *ad infinitum*, and poetasters write verses upon the beauties of Slavery, and its blessings to the slave among a peculiar and beloved people; but it is a subject *tabooed*, and forever, to the rest of mankind.

Men at the South who are not owners of slaves are looked upon as a set of poor insignificant "Bukra," who have not, or cannot, or ought not to have a stake in the soil, unless upon the condition of being the flunkies of slave-owners and executing Lynch-law upon every Abolitionist, every enemy of human bondage. They must, each one, think, speak, and act in accordance with the wishes of his liege lord—some rich neighbor—and be fitted to the Procrustean bed of his moral proportions; or, proving intellectually and politically too expansive to suit the views of this lord, consigned to abandonment, exile, and ruin.

If vanity, the desire of notoriety, or even the honest love of fame, could at one time have urged the author of these poems to literary effort, that time, he begs to assure his readers, has forever passed away. Should fame through these pages commend him as a writer, she could only (probably) invest him with *posthumous* honors, or at best deck his temples at a period and under circumstances when he would not, to use the words of a very great man, "give a peck of refuse wheat" for all that the world calls glory.

With these prefatory remarks, the Author, gentle reader, rejoices in the hope that you will aid him, through these pages, in accomplishing an object most dear to his heart,—the emancipation from slavery among demi-savages of those two worthy, though humble persons, referred to in the following Dedicatory Tale, ODERICK AND MILLY.

INTRODUCTION.

"THERE are those who take the name of Christians, and yet cling to the practice of making their fellow-creatures an article of commerce. Some delude themselves with the idea that they can ameliorate the condition of those over whom they have usurped this unlicensed power; but forget that he who *begins* to be a *slave, ceases* to be a *man;* that slavery is the extinction of our nobler part, and the abuse even of that part in us which we have in common with the brutes. Slavery in its most aggravated form—bondage—adds to the loss of personal liberty, cruel treatment."—CRABBE.

Durum nimis jugum tyranni.

"Flee from the rage
Of *cruell will,* and see thou kepe the *free*
From the foul yoke of *sensual bondage.*"
WYAT.

"I have nothing at his hands for my service but blows; when I am cold he heats me with beating; when I am warm he cools me with beating; I am waked with it when I sleep, raised with it when I sit, driven out of doors with it when I go home, welcomed home with it when I return; nay, I bear it on my shoulders, as a beggar wont her brat."—SHAKSPEARE'S *Com. Err.,* Act iv., Scene iv.

"I have struggled through much discouragement, and much opposition, much obloquy, much calumny, for a people with whom I have no tie but the common bond of mankind."—BURKE.

"'This is God's curse on slavery! a bitter, bitter, most accursed thing! a curse to the master and a curse to the slave! I was a fool to think I could make any thing good out of such a deadly evil. It is a sin to hold a slave under laws like ours. I always thought so when I was a girl. I thought so still more after I joined the church, but I thought I could gild it over. I thought by kindness, and care, and instruction, I could make the condition of mine better than freedom! fool that I was!'

"'Why, wife! you are getting to be an Abolitionist quite.'

"'Abolitionist! If they knew all I know about slavery, they might well talk!

INTRODUCTION.

we do not need them to tell us. You know I never thought that slavery was right, never felt willing to own slaves.'

"'Well, then you differ from many wise and pious men. You remember Mr. B.'s sermon, the other Sunday?'

"'I do not want to hear such sermons; I never wish to hear Mr. B. in our church again. Ministers can't help the evil, perhaps can't cure it, any more than we can; but defend it! it always went against my common sense; and I think you did not think much of that sermon, either.'

"'Well,' said Shelby, 'I must say these ministers carry matters further than we poor sinners would exactly dare to do.'"—*Uncle Tom's Cabin*, vol. i., chap. v. (1852), p. 58.

"Tell me not of rights; talk not of the property of the planter in his slaves. I deny the right; I acknowledge not the property. In vain you tell me of laws that sanction such a claim. There is a law above all the enactments of human codes, the same throughout the world, the same in all times. It is the law written by the finger of God in the hearts of men; and by that law, unchangeable and eternal, while men despise and loathe rapine, and abhor blood, they shall reject with indignation the wild and guilty phantasy that *man* can *hold property* in *man*."
—BROUGHAM.

"I can never cease to be most unfeignedly thankful that I was not born in a land of slaves. No one can understand the effect of the unutterable meanness of the slave system on the minds of those who, but from the strange obliquity which prevents them from feeling the degradation of not being gentlemen to pay for services rendered, would be equal in virtue to ourselves. Fraud becomes as natural to them as paying one's way is to the rest of mankind."—LIVINGSTONE'S *Travels*, p. 39.

"Many politicians in our time are in the habit of laying it down as a self-evident proposition, that no people ought to be free till they are fit to use their freedom. The maxim is worthy of the fool in the old story, who resolved not to go into the water till he had learned to swim. If men are to wait for liberty till they become wise and good in slavery, they may wait forever."—MACAULAY'S *Miscellanies.—Milton*, p. 13.

> "Goe, little booke, thyself present,
> As child whose parent is unkent;
> And when thou art past jeopardee,
> Come tell me what was said of mee,
> And I will send more after thee."
>
> SPENSER.

DEDICATORY TALE.

ODERICK AND MILLY.

Early trials. Native States. First owners. Separation. Reunion as the property of a benevolent man; after whose death they fall into the hands of a tyrant. Attempt to escape. Capture. Punishment. Present condition. Object of these rhymes their liberation.

I.

WHILE young, their souls were knit in one,
    Nor knew they how to part;
The grief that Oderick would own,
    Oft rent his Milly's heart.
An Indian claimed poor Oderick,
    A white man owned his wife;
Those men (kind masters) were alike
    Averse to wrath and strife.

II.

Change to our lowly friends ensued;
    A caitiff purchased both,
Who only *self* in all things viewed,
    Nor was to part them loth.
Dragged from her husband and her child,
    The trial Milly bore
For three long years; but God beheld
    Her wrongs!—they met once more.

III.

Both, taken to a good man's home,
    There till his death abode,

DEDICATORY TALE.

Nor ever thought from him to roam,
    Nor fate nor fortune chode.*
Next, as their owner, is declared
    One who, in harshness schooled,
Nor black nor white folks ever spared,
    By angry passions ruled:

IV.

One, too, miscalled a man of God,
    A preacher of His word;
But better named, a scourge, a rod,
    A scorpion, or a sword:
One who his country has for gold,
    His conscience, and his friends—
Yea! would his hopes of heaven have sold
    To serve his private ends:

V.

An old-school Presbyterian late,
    A bigot New-Light now;
Austere, morose, with Choctaw pate,
    A buffle head and brow.
Decided by his views of gain
    And grace! this church he found
To suit him, scriptural and plain,
    And on slave chattels sound.

VI.

These felt his ire, and sought by flight
    From bitter bonds to flee;
But, captured, manacled, and beat,
    Bewail their misery!

---

* *Chode*, the old preterite of *chide*. "And Jacob was wroth, and *chode* with Laban," Gen. xxxi. 36. Again, Numbers xx. 3: "And the people *chode* with Moses."

DEDICATORY TALE.

Their capture happened in this wise—
It is a tristful tale!—
The woman donned a boy's disguise—
They took an Indian trail.

VII.

Her side-long saddle she retained,
But changed her name to Billy,
And rode as women are constrained
By mode! Sad mode for Milly!
Her party numbered four in all,
One white, and negroes *three*,
Now flying fast from cruel thrall,
Arkánsas slavery.*

VIII.

A trader marked her horse's gear,
And raised a hue and cry;
Poor Milly's looks (half dead with fear)
Soon solved the mystery.
John Crabtree was the trader hight,
A coarse and burly brute;
His very name imports a wight
Of bitter bark and fruit.

IX.

With armed men and boys and hounds,
To bind them hand and foot,
This knave the little group surrounds,
Who, rather than be shot,
Submit themselves again to be
Consigned to savage slavery.

---

* The people of Arkansas generally accent the penultimate, as in the text.

DEDICATORY TALE.

X.

Long they beheld the cursed spot
    Whereon their blood was poured;
The stocks, the paddles, and the knout;
    The man they most abhorred.
Ay! more than stocks or whips accurst,
    Or dogs that lapped their blood,
Was HE, in hateful memory first—
    That minister of God!
Now hired to *him* who writes these lays,
    And *serving faithfully*,
He by this *little book essays*
    To *buy* and *set them free*.

XI.

Kind, gentle reader, pray regard!
    In this, his humble muse,
It needs must be his best reward
    That thou his rhymes diffuse.
Their PROFIT, *profit* should there be,
    To Afric we devote,
An offering meet to Liberty!
    Go, sail our little boat!

XII.

May favoring gales, through reefs and rocks,
    Impel thine onward course,
And steer thee clear of all the shocks
    Of treachery and force;
Or drift thee to some sheltered place
    Where tempests never blow,
And angels! ministers of grace,
    Keep watch upon thy prow.

XIII.

If once, thou fragile little bark!
    Thou touch the British Isles,
Or Britain's gracious sovereign mark
    Thy tiny sails with smiles,
Thou still, though vexed and tempest-tossed,
    Wilt jubilantly ride
Through ocean, sea, and rocky coast,
    In triumph o'er the tide;
Or safely anchor'd in some cove
    Of this our Empire State,
Thou mayest the little book, in love,
    Send forth to try its fate.
Thy mission, bond-slaves to unloose,
    The exile to restore,
To bring to wearied hearts repose,
    And fetter lawless power.

CHIVALRY AND SLAVERY.

IN EIGHT CANTOS.

CANTO I.

ANALYSIS.

Capture of negroes in Africa. No need of fiction. Slavery at home. Slave piracy as it now exists. American ports at which slaves are landed. Diseases on board slavers. Inexpressible horrors. Death-scenes. Conclusion of Canto I.

I.

Who from a slave-ship dares to borrow
Its history of human sorrow,
Or touches on the first assault,
The flight, the rout, the conquest, halt—
The dragging from the land to shore
Of all they loved or could adore—
From freedom, children, homes, and wives,
To woe and slavery and gyves—
Of trembling captives; how they sink
To earth, as, on the very brink
Of utter ruin, they implore
Mercy from those who ne'er before,
Or *then*, to cries of mercy listened,
Or marked the tear-drops as they glistened
In eyes that ne'er again may see
The glorious sun of liberty!
Or who *home* slavery essays
To make the subject of his lays,
May well a heavenly muse invoke,
As one involved in mist and smoke

Would pray for an unerring light,
His stumbling steps to plant aright,
His heart to warm, his spirit fire,
And quicken every good desire,
That while, in all his soul's revealings
And all his sympathetic feelings,
   Such dreadful records pass before him,
He may not, from the truth abating,
Or, for effect, a fact misstating,
One jot or tittle add; and see,
For thus infringing verity,
   The sword of vengeance hanging o'er him!

II.

Ah me! what need is there of fiction,
When it is found past contradiction
That on this point no fiction reaches
What the most truthful record teaches
Of horrors multiplied on horrors,
In all their dark and hideous colors?
Horrors enough there are at home,
Where'er in Southern States we roam;
But what in Africa we trace
To the dishonor of our race,
Be first our song. By law abolished,
Nations esteemed among the polished,
'Tis said, slave-traffic still connive at.
Slavers such daring skill arrive at,
That, *maugre* prohibition laws,
And Argus eyes and lions' claws,
Along the line of Afric's coast,
There are who often make their boast
That they, of treaties contraband,
Bring human cargoes to our land,

CHIVALRY AND SLAVERY.

Or *parts* of *cargoes*. What the rest
Befalls, it is by all confessed,
Those and those only best narrate
Who've witnessed their unhappy fate.

III.

Texas, Peru, Brazil, and Cuba!
How dreadful to the sons of Juba!
Matters it if they reach Aranzas,
Or come to anchor at Matanzas,
Or Arequipa or Truxillo,
Para, Callao, Mazanillo,
Iquiqui, Arica, Guasco,
Bahia, Rio, San Francisco,
Or at the mouth of Pearl River,
Accursèd now, accurst forever;
Or at that Mississippi jetty,
Dubbed, as *par excellence*, a *city*,*
Not by the rule of a *crescendo*,
But *lucus* like *a non lucendo*;
Or, lower down, at Pascagoula,
Or Timbalier or Pensacola,
Or Barataria or Biloxi,
Black Bay, Perdido, Choctawhaxi,
Vermilion Inlet, or Côte Blanche,
Or in that Mississippi branch,
Atchafalaya, or Sabine,
Or any other place between.

IV.

Or in thy wards, Floridian Key!
Or Georgian Isles to Ogeechee;

---

* Mississippi City, in the State of Mississippi, on the Gulf coast, has a court-house, some stores, two hundred and fifty inhabitants, and a good harbor. See *Harper's Gazetteer*.

CHIVALRY AND SLAVERY.

Or near the mouth of Great Pedee,
The vaunted home of chivalry;
Or Helen Sound or Beaufort Isle,
Through swamps and thickets to defile;
Or up to Edgefield, where one Brooks
Reigns paramount of bully *rooks;*
Or anywhere along that coast
Which *both* the *Carolinas* boast,
And old Virginia, up to Hampton,
By spider laws, less cramped than *Crampton.**

v.

While hurried inward from the strand,
The traders find for each a stand
In fields of sugar-cane, tobacco,
Grain, coffee, cotton, rice, or cocoa.
There, lashed in gangs, they end their days
In ceaseless toil or wild amaze;
Some, death preferring to submission,†
Perish from want in *manumission.*
Thus slaves are openly imported,
And for our markets classed and sorted,
With approbation and applause,
In utter scorn of all our laws!
Yet yield we not the right of search,
Or visitation, and would stretch
Our own immunities to knaves
Whose *only commerce is in slaves.*

---

* The webs of diplomatic texture by which Mr. Crampton was snared must be fresh in the recollection of the reader.

† A young and esteemed friend, from Texas, reports the case of a poor native African, who, landed from a piratical vessel, fled to the woods from his captors, preferring, like hundreds of his race, starvation and death to the bread and the bitterness of bondage. Others are spoken of as so unconquerable that their purchasers suffer them to depart, or send them away.

VI.

To loathsome dungeons chained, confined,
Hundreds on hundreds are consigned
In slave-ships. Cohorts of diseases
Appear, and each its victim seizes.
Scurvy, the meanest of the throng
   Of foul eruptions, widely spread
The hapless sons of men among,
   Here all its subjects counts as dead.
There *fever* drinks the tide of life—
A few more tossings end the strife.
Small-pox, confounding every feature,
Leaves not a trace of human nature,
Or nought except a putrid mass
Of what a human body was.
Perhaps a cry of execration
On all this foul and deep damnation
Escapes from lips that burst asunder:
Nor surely need we greatly wonder
That they who to the sin of color
And love of the almighty dollar
Owe all their woes, should curse and hate
The men who brought them to this state.

VII.

Better those fierce sirocco blasts
Should rend their sails and snap their masts,
And whelm them in the boiling deep
   Till the last trumpet's sounds awake them—
Better an everlasting sleep
(If such there were), than thus to be
The prey of such wild agony—
   The fears, the throes, the pangs that rack them.
What muse can sing, what tongue can trace,
The awful horrors of that place?

What heart conceive the sighs and groans,
The low, despairing monotones,
Of dying men, in masses spread
Upon the bodies of the dead?
With matted hair and wan despair,
And haggard eyes and dreadful cries,
And poisoned breath, the smell of death,
Some call aloud for those they love,
   While others, trembling, faltering, fearing,
   Confused alike in sight and hearing,
Ask pitying mercy from above!
No friend is near to calm their fear,
   No suns arise on wings of healing;
     Around their bed no tear is shed
   Of sorrowing love or kindly feeling;
No pious prayer, religion's care,
Is breathed to lift their souls to heaven;
   No sound is heard of that blessed word
Which speaks, through Christ, of sins forgiven.
The cry for drink upon the brink
   Of life's fast ebbing sands, so needed,
     Meets no regard—it is not heard,
   Or heard, is cruelly unheeded!
The swollen tongue, unnerved, unstrung,
   Parched, stiffened, from the mouth protruding,
Locked fast in death, impedes the breath,
   All hope of ease or life precluding.
Such is this hell of souls unbless'd,
Of heaving waves and wild unrest,
Of Gorgon dreams and doleful sounds,
Of fetid steams and gangrened wounds—
A tragic drama thronged with spectres,
Infernal hypocrites the actors.*

---

* The writer of this poem met, some years back, in one of the lower parishes

CHIVALRY AND SLAVERY.

When plunged into the foaming deep,
The curtain falls on those who sleep
In death: their shroud and grave and dirge,
The trough and thundering of the surge!
Yet *happier far* who thus find graves
In ocean's deepest, darkest caves,
Than those who *live* to *serve* as *slaves!*

CANTO II.

ANALYSIS.

Some instances of cruelty. Separation. Punishments. Pitch pine kindled on the lacerated flesh. Flogging with a saw. Crushing to death in a cotton-press. Rolling and flogging on a barrel. A beardless Nero. An incarnate devil. Teeth punched out with mallet and chisel. Washington and Lafayette, Slaves. Mutilation. Eaten up by worms. Financial policy of H. in the purchase of slaves. Fiasco with one arm. The centipede. Description. The higher law. The Missionary Hymn. The child. Bishop Heber. Greek and Roman Poets. Homer. Hesiod. Corinne. Sappho. Virgil. Horace. Ovid. Hebrew poets. Christian Fathers. Te Deum. Lord Macaulay. Addison and other writers of sacred song.

I.

At home, we might such facts disclose,
So full of horrors and of woes,
As, unrecorded in a court,
Would challenge faith in our report;
How well soe'er it may consort,

of Louisiana, a Virginia slave-pirate, just landed with his cargo of *souls*. He had long before seen him on board a Norfolk (Va.) steamer, with a number of negroes chained together, on their way to the human flesh market of Georgia. If fisheries be a school for sailors, is not domestic slavery a school of African slave-piracy? The re-establishment or sanction by the law of nations of the African slave-trade is strenuously advocated by Governor Alston, of South Carolina, and by many of the delegates of late Southern Conventions. Some of them regard it as "one of the greatest missionary enterprises the world ever saw!"

CHIVALRY AND SLAVERY.

With what is oft the fate of slaves,
From earliest childhood to their graves.
The butcher, who purveys our veal,
Will from the cow her offspring steal,
Nor cares though she the valleys fill
With piteous lowings, if he still,
At wonted marketable price,
Make good his every-day supplies;
Nor cares the purchaser of slaves,
   The infant from its mother's breast,
     The brother from the sister weeping,
The father, mother, husband, wife,
To drag and separate for life.
   They look in vain for peace or rest;
In distant States they find their graves,
     Sorrows on sorrows ever heaping.

II.

It chanced that in a Southern State,
Which one 'twere bootless to relate,
Two slaves were, under the pretense
Of some—by no means grave—offense,
Pinned down and fastened to the ground,
Their backs by scourging made one wound;
Then on the bleeding, mangled flesh
Were knots of pitch-pine, cut afresh,
Ignited: each to each was near,
The bubbling blood-streams to ensear;
Nor till the tortured victims died,
Were wrath and vengeance satisfied.
The overseer, and not the master,
Was the foul cause of this disaster;
In *sham arrest,* he broke *parole!*
The guilt lies still upon his soul,

His body safe: for Alabama,
Or for the coast of the Grand Lama,
For aught we know, he left; we leave him.
Can he repent, so Heaven forgive him!!
What the unpardonable sin is,
Not very easy to explain is:
Some say the callousness of Pharaoh,
And some the cruelty of Nero,
Some one thing say, and some another;
But though the point excite such pother,
The sin, we think, is found in *both*—
In *Rome* and *Egypt*, *will* and *oath*—
Cause and *effect, combined* in *one*,
A cruel will, a heart of *stone!*

III.

Bound down and pinioned, as we've stated,
Another (so *authenticated*)
O'er the stark bodies of his slaves
With threats and furious vengeance raves;
Flatways a saw descending hacks
And lacerates their subject backs,
By atmospheric pressure denting
The stricken part; thence raised by force,
It scatters in its upward course,
A mince of dripping flesh and blood!
Can such atrocities, O God!
Begin, thy *lightning* not *preventing?*
The wretch who thus his negroes treated,
Had all such chattels sequestrated,
And by an act of legislation
Condemned, disfranchised, by the nation
Or State (we rather should have said),
Is now *politically dead!*

IV.

Two hands beneath a cotton-press
Were placed; the *martyr*—was he less?—
Thus left all night to writhe in pain,
Lived till the morning dawned again.
Enters the master: his poor slave
Now turns his head relief to crave.
"What! damn you! grin," the tyrant cries,
"*In* with him; *press!*" The victim sighs
His last brief litany, and dies!

V.

We knew a youth, his name was Daves,
His father owned a score of slaves—
It may be more, it may be less;
We might in either acquiesce,
Although to have them *overrated*
Gives less offense than *understated*.
No man of property so proud as
He who of slaves a numerous crowd has;
So true it is men often *boast*
Of that which ought to shame them most.
Our youth was graduate of a college,
And had, 'twas thought, imbibed some knowledge—
Not a great deal, we may presume,
Nor think it too much to assume
That graduating is no test
Infallible of what is best,
Or for the body or the soul,
As evidenced in self-control,
Or rather *want* of it, in schools
Where rods ne'er reach the backs of fools!

VI.

By power, licentiousness and drink,
This hopeful hero had, we think,

His head and heart alike corrupted.
One act of his is here reported:
He tutored thus his overseer,
His negroes' flesh with whips to tear:
" Rise on your feet, as I on mine—
You so a better purchase gain—
Then, jerking, bring the thong toward you;
The practice soon will well reward you!"

VII.

On whisky-cask, bound down with rope,
And *taut* as any iron hoop,
He rolled a hapless slave around,
His back one wide and ghastly wound,
His blood fast streaming to the ground.
The tyrant's dogs, without control,
Lap fiercely up the crimson pool,
While bellowing cattle spurn the gutter,
Infuriate, as from scent of slaughter.
The beardless Nero sank exhausted,
So long the sickening torture lasted:
He sank, we said, but soon upstarted,
And to the whisky-bottle darted.
Thence, quick returning, he renewed
His work of blood; but what ensued?
How long the victim lived we know not,
And what we know not, we avow not;
But *this* we know, that, bending double,
His after life was pain and trouble;
He rather crawled than walked as man,
Till death released him from his pain.
And *this* we *know*, his wicked master,
 Or urged by drink or something worse,
From crime to crime went fast and faster,
 Till *suicide* cut short his course.

CHIVALRY AND SLAVERY.

Thy snow-white cotton, Carolina,
Was blood-stained by this fell hyena!

VIII

Brained by the kicking of an ass—
Let other circumstances pass—
The *when*, the *where*, the *special how ;*
Suffice it we the *means* avow,
And that in all *Death's* armory,
No shaft so suited our Legree—
Was W. H., whom, to be civil,
We would not call " incarnate devil !" *
If he had not such acts committed,
As " Moloch homicide" had fitted,
And Satan we believe outwitted.
His mode of punishment was this :
Whene'er he fancied aught amiss,
Chisel and mallet, both in hand,
He quickly uttered the command,
" Open your mouths, hold fast your breath,
Till I have punched out your d——d teeth !"
Poor Washington, we knew him well,
And Lafayette this fate befell ;
From curses, oaths, and imprecations,
Legree such horrid mutilations
Wrought on their bodies, as no pen
Can dare describe. O Heaven ! and when,
While yet alive and both in chains,
The worms devouring their remains ;—
Not half remained, save skeleton,
Of Lafayette and Washington—
In myriads crawled in every wound,
Where yet a loathsome place was found ;

---
* Parlor and Cabin.

They cried for mercy: gibes and scoffs
Were mixed the more with stripes and cuffs.
Death came at last to end their woes.
But not our narrative to close,
The ice once broken, we more apt are
To write than not—another chapter.

IX.

I buy, said he, the old and feeble,
Whom other planters gladly part with
At a small price; I quickly treble,
The value of what thus I start with:
I calculate their length of days,
And all the produce they are able
Within that given time to raise;
And thus I make them profitable,
By *extra work*, in say, three years:
It may be more, 'tis sometimes less,
They sink, of course, into their graves;
But then, just mark how it appears:
My profit on the work that kills them
Enables me to buy *young slaves;*
My neighbors all declare it fills them
With sheer amazement—they confess
That I, with sixty hands, each day can
Thrice as much cotton *work* as *they* can
With the same number; do they lie?
No, no! our plans explain the *why:*
They use the *whip*, the *chisel*, I !

X.

Do look at Flasco, mark his work;
Light and elastic as a cork,
He's just the same at hoe or fork;
He lost his left arm in a gin,
To me it matters not a pin;

I make him do as all the rest,
And, as you see, they do their best;
Am I to suffer any harm,
Because that wretch has lost an arm?
At first he seemed disposed to linger
Behind his fellows; now my finger,
Held up in threatening to his cheek
Makes him forget that he is weak.
Use, my dear sir, you know makes master.
His work grows better, if not faster;
I've only left him a few grinders,
But they may serve as prompt reminders
Of what he may expect, if I
Think right the chisel to apply.
When I'm away, my overseer
Has whips and paddles on their rear.*

XI.

While chattering thus, and bottling wrath,
A *centipede* upon his path
Appeared; he lifted up his cane,
And dropped it on its end again,
Close to the reptile, near the hole
Which of its wanderings seemed the goal.
As by electric shock confounded,
Or by some other cause astounded,
An instinct of self-preservation,
Perhaps, pervading animation,
Wherever found, collapsed as dead,
The creature moved nor limb nor head

---

* Mr. Bledsoe, and all who quote the Bible to support Slavery, would do well to see how far such cruelty as this is countenanced by the law of Moses:

"If a man smites out his man-servant's tooth, or his maid-servant's tooth, he shall let him go free for his tooth's sake." Exod. xxi. c. v. 27.

For a few moments; "Look you! see!"
Said H.; "A law for *you* and *me*.
Deception, after all our toil,
Is what best makes the kettle boil.
That insect only *seemed* to die,
Suspecting that a foe was nigh;
Now *mark*, that when the danger's o'er,
'Twill run as nimbly as before."
And so it was; silence ensued,
The centipede its course pursued,
Surveying cautiously the ground,
And looking furtively around;
Or ere the eye could mark its flight,
It had evanished out of sight.
"This," H. resumed, "is nature's skill;
I call it but deception still.
The Jesuits understand it well,
And very justly make it tell
To their advantage; 'tis their rule,
And who gainsays it is a fool;
All means are right, whene'er the end
To one's self-interest may tend."

XII.

"There is," said B., "a higher law,
Our bestial instincts to o'erawe.
If you regard yourself as blest
In that a miscreant confess'd
You stand, or reptile, follow nature—
The only law of such a creature;
But if you would let reason guide,
Or by God's *written law* abide,
It would far different views instil,
Expand your mind, subdue your will."

"—— By George! that law wont do for me, sir;
'Twould make my niggers all go free, sir.
A law of that kind is but fustian—
I hope I ne'er may be a Christian!
A law of that kind is all nonsense,
It runs a-tilt against my conscience;
In short, sir, you are too dogmatical,
Though somewhat *radical*, not practical."
"Aye! *root* and *branch*," responded B.,
"Oppression, fraud, hypocrisy
I would uproot, and rescue slaves
From ruffian taskmasters and knaves,
And pray that God may soon convert
To love and truth each atheist heart!"

XIII.

"You have my daughter taught a hymn, sir—
A sort of stuff I much contemn, sir—
A Missionary hymn, I think;
I must not at such doings wink."
"The hymn," said B., "is Bishop Heber's;
I had supposed that if a Gheber's
Were couched in language so sublime,
You'd scarcely think it a foul crime
To make a little child repeat it.
What's your objection? Let me meet it."
"'Tis very old, sir." "You're mistaken;
It would in this sweet child awaken"—
"Sir, sir! tis you mistake, not I;
I've heard it in my infancy."
"Not you," said B., "you are as old
As he who wrote it——he is cold,
And has been some time in his grave,
An honored prelate and a brave,

CHIVALRY AND SLAVERY.

Whose spirit grieved to see a slave."
"Sir, you are personal." "Agreed—
It is precisely what you need.
But would you," B. pursued, "a hymn,
Because you think it *old*, condemn?"
"Yes, yes! I always like what's new,
And let me add, 'twixt me and you"—

*　*　*　*　*　*　*

XIV.

"There is," said B., "our friend, Dan Homer—
Pray do not think him a new-comer
Into these parts—he wrote some hymns
In noble measure, though not rhymes.
Our overseers might call him foggy,
And, drunk themselves, think Homer groggy.
Of better folks we've met with some
Who Homer's nods ascribe to Rum!
Old Hesiod, Homer's rival bard,
Had for the gods supreme regard.
His deathless book 'Of Works and Days'
In moral rules and songs of praise
Abounds; and his Theogony,
The birth of gods, called eke *Cosmogony*,
Like Moses', David's, Miriam's verses,
God's wonders in his works rehearses.
One Virgil, too, was 'up to snuff;'
The hymns he wrote were well enough.
A man named Pindar wrote some Peans,
Which few could rival in Orléans;*

---

* The factors and pettifoggers of the New Orleans slave-market, and the scribes of the pro-slavery press, were this creature's *ideals* of all mercantile and literary talents. The accent on the penult in Orleans is not unfrequent in the South.

CHIVALRY AND SLAVERY.

His hymns from ruin saved his house,
Perhaps his heirs, and eke his spouse.
Corinna, Sappho, women both,
Were, as your daughters, nothing loth
Some sacred poems to recite;
Few could like them, or read or write
Like Sappho,* muse of Mytylene,
And eke of Tanagra, Corinne.
The former added to the 'Nine,'
The latter scarcely less divine.
A Roman man, named little Horace,†
Would as a church-mouse be as poor as,
Were he not able to proclaim
In song, his god's and country's fame.
You have an Ovid in translation,
And know him well in illustration; ‡
Of his great art and transmutation
You need no sort of information—

---

* *Sappho* was called the *Tenth Muse*.
† Horace is regarded as the Poêt Laureat of Augustus. See *Carmen Seculare*, &c.
‡ Our hero was a great patron of this species of illustrative art. It is to be hoped his friends will not object to see himself well illustrated.

He was scarcely of middle height, with a tanned, Arab-shaped face and figure. He was lank-jawed, herring-gutted—had a forehead villanous low—sandy, excrementitious hair—whitish brows—sparse, swinish lashes of the same color, and *cruel gray eyes*, between which his nose—somewhat aquiline—formed an *isthmus* of marvellous tenuity, indicating, phrenologically, "*small size!*"

Veneration was wanting; benevolence, inappreciable; self-esteem, inordinate; destructiveness, monstrous. His hands were freckled, bony, lean, and long-fingered. He was sparrow-legged and splay-footed (slightly so); choleric, quick spoken; inarticulate and asthmatic. Passion had the same effect upon this jabberer as fear has upon others.

"*Steteruntque comæ, et vox faucibus hæsit.*"

Save this, mayhap, that he sometimes
Would to the gods address some hymns:
Isaiah, David, Job, and Moses,
From one who poetry composes,
Or values justly, for their lays
Are thought entitled to some praise."

XV.

" To *Ambrose* and *Augustine,* we
Who cherish no antipathy
To sacred songs, though e'er so old,
The hymn " *Te Deum*" are so bold
As to ascribe. Both men were true,
And great, perhaps, as I or you.
'Tis true Macaulay damns their Latin *

---

* The great historian has himself accounted for the inelegant Latinity of the declining empire, and comparatively new religion of Rome in the days of Augustine and Ambrose. But what is it in the present instance that offends Lord Macaulay's classical taste? Is it the Seraphim, Cherubim, and Sabaoth of the Sacred Writings? Has he forgotten that even Pollio and Mæcenas might have used *monoptots* in their own majestic vernacular? Or is it the phrase "*proclamant tibi Sanctus,*" that has induced him to lay his heavy hand upon a composition so sublime and venerable as the Te Deum?

Possibly the guests of Pollio and Mæcenas, of Cicero and Cæsar, would not—if Christians, or acquainted with the doctrines of Christianity—have been more shocked or perplexed by the technical phraseology of Ambrose and Augustine, had they lived in their time, than Lord Macaulay or Mr. Russell now are by some of the technicalities of Geology and other sciences, in the writings of certain living authors as eminent as themselves. Are the Almo Sol! Levis Illythia, Veraces, Parcæ, &c., of Horace, more sublime than the Sanctus, Sanctus Dominus Deus Sabaoth?

In the age to which Lord M. refers, and still more in subsequent ages, law and medicine had almost, if not quite, as large a share in the corruption and decline of the Latin tongue, as the technical language of Christian theology.

On the whole, there is much unprofitable pedautry in the discussion of the question as to the time when the golden age of the Latin tongue had ceased. If Vida,

As gibberish, rude and misbegotten,
Or fustian woven upon satin;
Yet scarce his own immortal lays,
Have won more unrestricted praise.
Transition, faith, as well as rock,
Must needs fastidious critics shock,
With words importing novel features,
As grafts on older nomenclatures:
In short, all sciences and schools,
Are fain to choose new words and rules,
Which, more or less, are innovations
On all the usages of nations;

Sannazarius, Bacon, Buchanan, Milton, Addison, Vincent Bournes, or the Marquis of Wellesley had written as good Latin verses as Horace (and in very many instances they are scarcely behind him), how few of our critics would dare to avow it!

"Though the classical Latin," says Dr. C. French, "had *salus* and *salvus*, it had not *salvare* nor *salvator*. The strong good sense of Augustine disposed of the difficulty. He made no scruple about employing *sa'vator*, observing, with a *true insight into the law of the growth of words*, that it was not good Latin before the Saviour came; but when He came, He made it to be such—for as shadows follow substances, so words result from things.

One of the very best authorities on this point is Lord Macaulay himself, who, in his review of the writings of Sir James MacIntosh, observes that Mr. Fox's extreme attention to the niceties of language was hardly worthy of so manly and capacious an understanding. He then proceeds to notice the censures of Horace upon the fastidiousness of the purity of Rome, and quotes Politian and Erasmus against unreasonable scrupulosity on that head.

"Ut bene currere non potest," says Politian, "qui pedem ponere studet in alienis tantum vestigiis, ita, nec bene scribere qui tanquam de præscripto non audet egredi."

"Posthac," exclaims Erasmus, "non licebit episcopos appellare patres reverendos, nec in calce literarum scribere annum a Christo nato, quod id nusquam faciat Cicero. Quid autem ineptius quam toto sæculo novato—religione, imperio, magistratibus, locorum vocabulis, ædificiis, cultu, moribus, non aliter audere loqui quam locutus est Cicero. Si revivisceret ipse Cicero, rideret hoc Ciceronianorum genus."

CHIVALRY AND SLAVERY.

Shall we then faith and science smother,
Or bear with one as well t'other?
Though more than Atticus condemn,
Abjure we not our noblest hymn!

XVI.

"One Addison, a man of taste,
Did not consider it a waste
Of time and talents to indite
Hymns which this child can well recite.
Young, Thomson, Milton, Moore, and Byron,
You doubtless value as old iron;
Nay, Tennyson and Browning, too,
Because as old as I or you."

XVII.

"Now what I mean I know full well,"
Said H., "I wish you all in h—l,
And wont be pestered any more
With your confounded musty lore."
B. wished his atheist host good night,
To chew his cud of wrath and spite.

CANTO III.

A vision. Cato, a slave. His terror and grief. His wife, children, and mother in Carolina. His horrible punishment and sufferings. Flight, pursuit, capture, death. Remonstrance. Inquest. Decomposition of the body of Cato. Reverses of H. Remorse of Cato's former owners. Reflections.

I.

Though early, B. wished to repair
Or to his couch or to his chair,
To meditate on what he'd seen
That day, or said, or heard, or been!

The moon was hid, the stars were dim,
The stillness, such as saddened him;
The air was close, he gasped for breath,
He seemed as in a house of death;
While thus he mused in gloomy mood,
A figure close behind him stood.
Its gentle breathing scarce the flix
Could agitate on infants' necks.
Not Priam, when, his curtain drawn,
He Troy in flames before the dawn
Beheld: nor Job, in dead of night,
As near him stood that dreadful sprite;
Nor who the locks and glaring eyes
Of gory Banquo saw arise;
Nor yet that Babylonian king,
As, revelling, and rioting,
His joints are loosened, and his knees
Smite one another as he sees
A hand in mystic figures scrawl
His swift destruction on the wall—
Had more of terror and amaze
Than B. at what now fixed his gaze.

II.

"In God's name! what are you?" he said,
"I'm Cato, mas'r, almost dead,"
The vision answered; "buy me, buy,
Or I this very night must die.
Hush! softly, he would kill me now,
If he could see me talk to you;
You knew old mas'r in Car'lina,
And missis, too, and old Aunt Dinah:
She is my mother. O sad day!
That brought me here, so far away!

Mas'r was young, and missis she
Had always sort of jealousy.
I was her coachman, footman, waiter—
She said she never had a better.
You knew my wife, she was their cook;
We had two children—one was Brook;
The little girl we called her Kitty—
You saw her, mas'r—wa'nt she pretty?
And we did love them both so dearly,
Mary and me did: we were nearly
The same in age; she was of me
As fond as I was fond of she.
Oh! it did almost break my heart,
To think that I from them should part.
And won't you write for me a letter,
To say I never loved them better
Than I do now? Do tell how strong
My wish to kind folks to belong,
Who would my children and my wife,
And me together buy for life.
But Mary now must have another.
More like a sister and a brother
We looked, as many people said,
Than man and wife—*I'm almost dead!*
Mary will never see me more,
Nor Brook nor little Kate deplore
My death; yet tell them, if I die,
That God will still take care of me;
That I will look down from above
On all below that share my love;
That I will watch their souls till God
Shall take them all to his abode;
That I shall pray for *them*, as *they*
Should pray for *me*, to meet that day

When the Great Judge shall in his book
Note every thought and every look,
And every wicked word and deed,
That makes a brother's heart to bleed."

III.

Poor Cato was a brown mulatto,
Still young in years. Alas! poor Cato!
Once very handsome, now his hair
All stood on end; his eyes would glare
With wild and preternatural light,
Like some ill-omened bird of night,
As he around the chamber glanced,
To see if any one advanced.
"They watch, me mas'r, watch me, fear
I should say something in your ear,
And which—oh! don't I know them well—
They do not wish that I should tell.

IV.

"Mas'r, this misery in my head,
Oh! it do feel so mighty bad!
He shot me here, he left me lying,
And thought—he did—I was a-dying:
The lead do make me heavy like—
See, feel, 'tis here the shot did strike,
Just in the back part of my skull,
Oh! it do make me mighty dull.
See here!" he opened wide his mouth,
His toothless gums revealed the truth,
Of teeth within that swollen face,
Mallet and chisel left no trace;
Black, bruised, his eyes were; and his nose
Was beaten flat with brutal blows.

V.

"Old mas'r, that is not the worst—
See, mas'r, here." "Oh! d—d, accursed
Villain," cried B., with sudden start,
And sobbed as if his very heart
Were breaking, breaking. "Oh my God!
Can these things be? and not Thy rod
Uplifted high this wretch to smite,
And cast him howling into night!"

VI.

Now B. consoled him all he could,
And promised faithfully he would
Use all his influence with the brute,
Who thus his vengeance dared to glut.
"Sooner," said H., "than Cato sell,
I'd see you all G—d d——d in h—l;
Now my revenge must have its turn,
And his black hide must bleed or burn."

VII.

That night poor Cato left the camp,
And sought a refuge in the swamp;
The game was up, the dogs were out,
And a few neighbors round about
Assisted in the deadly chase,
The hapless fugitive to trace.
Crossing an inlet where no hound
Could take the scent, poor Cato found
A little island; there, in vain,
He would his plans review again.
His wounds were fresh, his joints were sore,
Alas! for him no open door
Lay for escape in any quarter,
Where he might rest his head thereafter.

The dogs at fault upon the bank
He saw: his heart within him sank.
The Hunters came upon the bay,
Where now in view the islet lay.
" Cross, cross," said H., " this bay of islands ;
The villain has not sought the highlands.
If any see him, shoot him dead,
Though, blast him ! he's not worth the lead."
They cross ; and near a heap of bones,
The relics of some hogs and coons,
They saw him crouch : at once they fire.
Poor Cato did not yet expire ;
He lived some days—the fatal wound
Was in his side ; upon the ground,
Dying, he lay. A few suggest
A truck on which his weight might rest,
Till they conveyed him to the " quarters
Where they dispose of such deserters."

VIII.

" We've found him ; he is shot," said D.
" And who his murderer ?" cried B. ;
" Ho ! ho ! sir, you the act condemn ?"
" I do," retorted B. again.
H. took his knife and 'gan to grit
His teeth, and fiercely looked and spit.
" The blood which from that poor slave's wound,
Forth issues, coloring the ground
Shall rise in judgment to the throne
Of God, and draw due vengeance down
Upon your head, O wretched fool !
To bring such ruin on your soul,"
Said B. " I leave you—shall proclaim
Your cruel acts, your cruel name :

Aye, kill me! look that look again!
Your wrath I fear not, man of sin!
Repent you of this horrid crime,
While God in mercy grants you time."

IX.

B. when resolved all risks to brave,
Thus whispered to a neighbor's slave :
"When Cato's eyes in death are closed,
If you to me should feel disposed
To bring the news, I shall regard you,
And give five dollars to reward you."
Poor Cato had lain under ground
Long time, or e'er a single sound
Of his decease had reached the ears
Of B., who now had certain fears.
He notwithstanding called a jury
Of inquest: H. was in a fury.
Decomposition had set in,
And this time saved that man of sin.
Some one thing said, and some another,
And some resolved to act the brother;
H. threatened B. at sight to kill,
But feared to carry out his will,
Assured that Texas had no place
To save his neck in such a case.

X.

The man commissioned to bring word,
When he of Cato's death had heard,
Was told he should meet Cato's fate,
If he of such a thing should prate,
Or should to B. the news narrate.
What more ensued we may disclose
Some day at full, in verse or prose;

It was this caitiff's first disaster
To serve as steward a rigid master;
His cruel financiering failed him,
And to the counter basely nailed him.

XI.

Now Mary wept without control,
For grief lay heavy at her soul;
She blamed her owners as the cause
Of Cato's death, against all laws
Divine and human: they were bruised
And sore in spirit, and accused
Each other of a grave offense,
Against propriety and sense.
They parted; he his native shore
Beyond the ocean sought once more;
And she retained both land and slaves—
They both lie low in distant graves.
She treated Brook and Kitty kindly,
And was to Mary more than friendly;
She made them free in Carolina,
Where they are living with Aunt Dinah,
Where they will ever and anon
Cato lament and Washington,
And Lafayette, their youngest brother—
Aunt Dinah was of all the mother.

XII.

That eighty slaves, or even one,
Should be in such a miscreant's power
As IL, from twenty to require—
By age, disease, and work outworn—
What few from sixty could desire;
Or force by cruel lashes torn,
Should almost move a heart of stone,

CHIVALRY AND SLAVERY.

To consecrate each day and hour,
In every way the law allows,
To break their chains, their cause espouse ;
In short, to teach the holy creed,
That every human slave be freed.
Say that three thousand men like H.,*
In all our Slave States may be found—
That eighty hands, for every wretch †
Of such a stamp, must till the ground ;
A total eighty times three thousand
Results for field-work and for house, and—
All other objects to fulfil—
Lust, torture, wrath, a tyrant's will.

---

* When it is considered that there were in the United States, in 1850, 3,204,313 slaves, probably now (1860), 4,000,000, and that the number of families owning slaves was 347,525; that there are 2,000,000 in the relation of slaveowners, or about a third of the population of the Slave States; that, passing over smaller proprietors, 6,196 own 50 and under 100 slaves; 1,497, 100 and under 200; 187, 200 and under 300, &c. (see *Harper's Statistical Gazeteer*), it will be readily conceded that the writer of these rhymes has no disposition to exaggerate the statistics of cruelty, in supposing 240,000 slaves under merciless taskmasters like H.

To represent cases like those above described—as stale, exceptional, incredible, impossible, &c.—the hacknied accusations of lying and fanatical abolition scribblers—is a favorite topic of pro-slavery men. But alas! such cases are new every morning, and yet the same yesterday and to-day as they will ever continue to be under the tyrannous rule of a slave-irresponsible oligarchy.

† The end of H was worthy of his character. Ruined as a planter, on a false capital, he became, during the Mexican war, a trader in mules. One of these animals, infuriated by his cruelty, kicked off the roof of his skull. Hence, " brained by the kicking of an ass."

CANTO IV.

Wrath of the Southern people and the Southern press. Denial of alleged atrocities, how clearly soever proved. Legal abolition and the introduction of free labor, as cheaper and better, the only hope of a National expurgation from the curse of slavery. Instanced in Pennsylvania and New Jersey. Influence of the clergy. Incident to a clergyman traveling in Virginia.

I.

The South says, tell it not in Gath,
   Let hostile Ascalon not hear it !
Lest abolition on our path
   Should tread, and such abuses ferret,
As from an Institution spring,
Which to our marts such profits bring.
Nay, more : let's swear it is not true.
Who says he from plantations knew
Crimes so atrocious to transpire,
Let us avouch a reckless liar.

II.

Press, mallet and *chisel, saw, jackknife,* are weapons
Fit only for cotton-bags, lumber and capons !
From Picayune B——t to P——e the venal,
We all shall pronounce it a calumny penal ;
Men, of course, will reply, " see your own advertisements ;
If we are huge liars, 'tis oft by advisements
Of editors, planters, and mild overseers
(*How mild*, from their *threats* it most plainly appears),
Our noses to slit, and to crop off our ears.
These facts notwithstanding, let's treat them as fools—
The dupes of Ward Beecher, Lloyd Garrison's tools."

III.

Other horrors there are which produce a reaction;
But these we eschew. We are not of the faction
Who think that the slavery sanctioned by law
Can *without* law be banished from this generation,
Or even its discussion receive toleration
In our Southern States; for we always foresaw
That only free-labor, as cheaper and better,
Can from the poor slave strike his collar and fetter.
The Jerseys and Penn's State are pertinent cases :
    Their slaves were made free when free-labor grew cheaper,
    And no one desired to be always a keeper
Of paddles and chains to hold slaves in their places.
Perpend this, ye Know Nothings, maugre your creed,
If you wish that the blacks should from bondage be freed.

IV.

It may be the clergy would dare to attack,
    This compound of cruelty, fraud, and oppression;
A priest in a Slave State is only a hack,
    Whose place must depend on his cautious expression.
More gagged than the press, he must labor to teach
What on that point his patrons all wish him to preach ;
Or, at least, must keep silent on what he despises,
And drive from his flock abolition surmises ;
Those men have no chance who condemn the black code,
But to starve or subsist in some other abode,
Or loaf as Jack Puddings, whom famine impells
On Gunny-bags Harper and Baptist hard-shells !*

---

* It is truly marvellous that an editor with a respectable easy-chair, a table well furnished with excellent articles, fair literary notices, capital illustrations, &c., should produce from his drawer, as Harper does, the vapid tom-fooleries of Baptist hard-shells and the like illiterate *droles*. Other mouthlies, and all our great quarterlies, devoutly eschew such twaddle. It is not, however, the mere joking,

CHIVALRY AND SLAVERY.

In short, by slave-preaching to do any good
One's faith must, like Sumner's, be sealed with his blood; †

but the quality of the jokes we consider a fair subject for satire; and that their quality is, for the most part, beneath contempt, can scarcely escape the observation of those gentlemen themselves.

Surely there is genuine wit enough in the world, and accessible to the Harpers, to make manifest the needlessness, the detriment to good taste, and offense to sound scholarship, of overloading their columns, and surfeiting their readers with these messes of cold porridge from the drawer; but if new wit be lacking within the limits of a month, better is it far to resort at once to the conceits and frivolities of those standard professional jokers, Prentice & Co.

Strong, indeed, are the inducements held out to the Harpers to continue the bad practice referred to, for most of their readers, we are told, begin at the end of their periodical to search for their own or their neighbor's shame, in this species of lunacy; and many, no doubt, are subscribers and patrons for the consideration of seeing themselves in print. But is it not dangerous and pernicious to minister to a pruriency so pitiful? We have constantly present to our mental and, alas! bodily eyes, a tribe of feeble and stupid punsters, whom we regard as by no means the least of the many social evils we know of.

We wish well to the Harpers, and to the noble cause in which they are engaged, and to which they have done, and are still doing, distinguished service; but we pray that it may not be retarded by these pestilent small humorists, the greatest drawbacks imaginable to sound reasoning and general progress.

Finally, if the Harpers wish to increase the general circulation of their monthly, they must abstain from attacks, whether founded in ignorance or inspired by malice, upon the first lady in Christendom. The day of such small things, gentlemen, has passed away, and we trust forever, from the American public.

† Obscure individuals are, for the free expression of their sentiments upon slavery, treated, from time to time in the Southern States, as fanatical vagabonds; and mercilessly lynched by the most *vociferous celebrators of the Anniversary of Independence*. But it requires such illustrious victims as Charles Sumner to help essentially the cause of freedom, and to establish the truth of the aphorism, "*Sanguis martyrum, semen Ecclesiæ.*"

Such men as Cyprian, Justin, and Polycarp, did more for Christianity by their confession as martyrs than thousands of inferior note, how zealous soever in the cause of truth. Could a band of devoted clergymen be now found to preach the abolition of slavery in our Southern States, as Moses and Aaron preached it in

CHIVALRY AND SLAVERY.

At least he must count on most cruel extremes
From those whose strange gods he both hates and contemns.
A clergyman traveling once in Virginny,
Most feelingly spoke of the sons of New Guinea
Oppressed in our midst : " Stop the stage, stop the stage !"
Loud shouted the passengers, bursting with rage ;
" Who slanders a freeman and sides with a slave,
Is a cursed Abolitionist, traitor, and knave."
When dragged from the stage to be instantly lynched,
And like a vile Caliban cruelly pinched,
One well known to fame promptly came to his aid,
Assuring the crowd that the man so suspected

Egypt, as the Apostles and their followers preached it throughout the world, they would, doubtless, in very many instances find such preaching a short road to slander, extrusion, imprisonment, and death, but would do more by it to put an end to slavery than can be done by all the books, money, and speeches expended, or to be expended upon its abolition in all other sections of our Union or of Christendom.

As respects the alleged evils of such doctrine to the lives and fortunes of planters, and other white people in the South, we believe that the preaching of it in prudence and faithfulness would tend greatly to prevent or avert those evils, which, from the state of things, as now existing, must sooner or later ensue, or sudden visitations, as on Egypt ; or a Federal disunion, as in Greece ; or both, perhaps, with servile insurrection and massacre superadded, as in Rome and St. Domingo. We are now in the South, as we must be, till slavery be abolished, sleeping on the brink of a smouldering volcano.

" *Ignes suppositos cineri doloso !*"

" The Church must take the slave by the hand," says the Bishop of Oxford, " and, owning him as one of Christ's body, must lead him into the family of man. Not that she is bound to preach insurrection and rebellion. Far from it. It is quite easy to enforce upon the slave his duties under a system, the unrighteousness of which is, at the same time, clearly stated. His bonds are illegal ; but it is God's arm, and not his own violence, which must break them. Let the clergy of the South preach submission to the slave, if, at the same time, they declare to his master that those for whom Christ died are now no longer slaves, but brethren beloved ; and that a system which withholds from them their Christian birthright

CHIVALRY AND SLAVERY.

Was himself a *slaveowner*, though one not afraid
To say what he thought, and was highly respected
In a neighboring State, to which State he was going,
To see how his slaves and his cotton were doing.

INTRODUCTION AND ANALYSIS OF RHYMES.

BY A FRIEND.

CANTO V.

Sunrise. Scenes in a bar-room. In a Court-House. Judge, Lawyers, Jurors, Legislators, in the days of Judge Marshall and Goosequills. Judge Predom's opening address. Deportment. The prisoner. Clerk. Witness. Lawyer Jones' speech. Lawyer Pryor's speech. Summing of the evidence. Scripture text. St. Paul. Remarks which he might make if now living, and the case were brought before him. A reference to G. Smith and other celebrated abolitionists. The jury disagree. Summary vengeance by the populace. Examination of the judge's argument. Bledsoe's book. His profundity so much greater than that of other well-known authors. Locke, Blackstone, Montesquieu, and Burke, Hall, Whewell, Paley, Wayland, Channing. Scriptural arguments, &c.

I.

While pricking thus our wingèd horse,
A friend observant of our course
Asked, If, by way of episode,
We would a narrative or ode
Of his insert among our lines?
Preferring labor in those mines

---

is utterly unlawful; that it is one which the master, not the slave, is bound to set himself honestly to sweep away. Above all should they, at any cost, and by any sacrifice, protest in life and by act against this grievous wrong. The greater the cost, and the more painful the sacrifice, the clearer will be their testimony, and the more it will avail. To them it is given not only to believe in Christ, but also to suffer for His sake."—*Reproof of the American Church, Harned, New York*, 1846.

CHIVALRY AND SLAVERY.

Wherein ourselves, as Heaven's free gift,
Our drossier ore compound and sift,
Yet could we not with grace refuse,
The free-will offering of his muse;
And therefore, with inverted comma,
Produce his change of rhythmic *broma*.
There are who relish its *aroma*,
And think it worthy a *diploma*,
Relating still to old Virginny,
And the dark offspring of New Guinea:—

II.

" 'Twas early on a day in June,
The stars had vanished with the moon,
The full-orbed potent god of day,
Nature to clothe in bright array,
Was just prepared his course to run,
And scale the distant horizon.*
Once fairly entered on his track,
He waltzed along the zodiac.
The road was dry, the weather still,
When he the summit of yon hill
Had reached: he stopped, and looking down,
Beheld the bustle of our town,
And as the tavern bar was near,
Just in the path of his career,
Or seemed so—as its figure threw
Its shade athwart the glittering dew—
However occupied elsewhere,
His chief attention centred there.

---

* Our moon's eclipsed, and the occidental sun
Fights with old Aries for his *horizon*.
            See *Richardson's Dictionary*.

He saw the table, hearth and floor,
With various ruins covered o'er;
Boxes and dice were scattered round,
A pack of cards bestrewed the ground;
In wild confusion lay spittoons,
As stamped by boot-heels of dragoons,
And mantling pools of salivation,
Proclaimed the freedom of the nation;
Ejected *quids* and stump cigars,
Looked up the chimney at the stars,
As if rejoicing they were free,
From lips defiled with blasphemy—
From lips that still defile their embers,
Tongs, hearthstones, andirons and fenders,
Or what there is in shape of cinders,
As many a traveling wight remembers.
Decanters, pitchers, broken glasses,
Had of wild orgies left grim traces;
Men still were at the bar-room roaring,
While negro boys around lay snoring;
When each had drivelled o'er his dew-lap,
His *quantum suff.* of honey julep,
And breakfasted, so says report,
As 'twas agreed, they trudged to court,
A grave deportment all assuming,
While far and near the air perfuming
With Yankee rum and applejack,
Made by receipt of Almanac.

III.

Renowned for justice, law, and freedom
Of manner, sat our Justice Predom.
The lawyers right in front appear,
Each with his own peculiar leer;

The sheriff, somewhat in a hurry,
Called and impanellèd a jury.
And in the intermediate space
Between the judge and populace,
Sheriff and jury take their place.
'Twas at a time when men used goosequills,
And on their pantaloons wore *moose frills.*
'Twas in the time of corduroys,
And shocking hats, when the b'hoys
Did as they pleased in old Virginny,
And still imported slaves from Guinea;
When rival limbs of legislature
Seemed much improved in every feature
Of the inward and the outward man,
By change of garb—a blameless plan,
In those who only once a year
Can at the State's expense appear,
To sport their toggery in town,
And on the less distinguished frown.
Short triumph! sure as death and taxes,
The man who thus vain-glorious waxes,
How high or low his pedestal,
Is destined soon to have a fall,
Political or physical.

IV.

As rays proceeding from the sun,
Spread warmth and life from morn till noon,
And from the noon to dewy eve,
Yet nothing lose by what they give;
Even so our State's centralization,
Its light diffuses through the nation,
Maturing science, truth, and power,
Which, every day and every hour

Increasing, spread, reflexive shine,
Or on the sea or in the mine,
Or in the forge, or in the shop,
On hill, or vale, or mountain-top,
On river, railroad, and canal,
Or, in one word, to sum up all,
The *moral* and *material*.
Our Congressmen, or met from Maine,
From California, or the plain
Of Utah, Oregon, or Kansas,
Or round our seaboard from Aransas,
Or higher up to Arizona,
Nevada, Laramie, Colona,
Superior, or where'er we own a-
N embryo State, or read in story
Of some great Western territory,
Or peak, or pass, or bluff, or digging,
Or inlet, dotted o'er with rigging;
Or say some district like Dacotah—
Though late without a single vote: a
Realm of future Romes and Catos,
Of Homers, Xenophons, and Platos,
Of Hannibals, and Alexanders,
Of Shakspeares, Terences, Menanders,
Of Newtons, Bacons, Franklins, Lockes,
Of merchant-princes, skilled in stocks;
Of Austins, Chrysostoms, and Barrows,
Safe guides in theologic narrows;
Of Galens, Coopers, Motts, and Larrys,
Of Humboldts, Taylors, Kanes, and Parrys,
Pugins, Palladios, and Ruskins;
Of Liston socks, and Garrick buskins;
Of Raphaels, Angelos, and Titians;
Of men renowned among Venetians,

Like Giorgio Del Castel Franco,
Impressive as the ghost of Banquo,
Of Haydens, Handels, and Mozarts,
Brunells, in engineering parts;
And some like Morse, to whom 'tis given
To guide the lightning drawn from heaven;
Of Broughams, Marshalls, Sydenhams, Storys,
And Bunyan's far-famed allegories;
Of Livys, Bancrofts, and Macaulays,
Prescotts, and Liebigs, to whom all is
Assigned the task to teach the masses,
With Miller, Cuvier, Agassiz,
Watt, Fulton, Peel, Jackuard, and Arkwright,
McCormick, Whitney, Hargreaves, Cartwright—
Brothers who, in far-distant homes,
Design or take from Eastern domes
The new improvements in our looms,
Our agriculture, dwellings, docks;
Our roads, our aqueducts, and locks;
Our fashions, habits, social rules;
Our books, our sciences, and schools;
Nay, oft their teachers overtake,
And mighty impulses awake,
Which as the lightning from the pole,*
Pervade the heart, the life, the soul
Of every man in every place,
Within our commonwealth's embrace.

v.

Our patent-office, as a school,
We scarce sufficiently extol,
Of scientific skill and art,
The soul, the spirit, and the heart—

---

* The point or points in a magnet, in which the magnetic force is concentrated.

Not hampered much in execution,
By endlessness of collocution,
Or functional circumvolution.*
Our Barnacles must find a way
To do a thing without delay,
Or else into oblivion pack,
And never venture to come back.
But this we find is a digression
On centro-lateral progresssion;
The march, in triplicate alliance,
Of art, civility, and science.
Return we back to old Virginny,
And slaves imported from New Guinea.

VI.

'Twas when Judge Marshall in his glory
Of law and wisdom sat before ye,
Ye men of Richmond! ere your hall
Had heard or Black or Blanco bawl,
Like Allienus: † not a word
They uttered could be plainly heard.
They sought, as others do, applause
By strength of lungs and strength of jaws,
Not from their arguments or cause.
Silence proclaimed, " We now begin."
Our judge, from nibbling at his pen,
Did of the silence soon avail him;
But lest his memory should fail him,

---

* *Circumvolution*—as good a word, perhaps better, than that used by Dickens, " Circumlocution."

† Deinde ut opinor habet Allienum. In clamando quidem video cum esse bene robustum et exercitatum.—*Cicero in Quintum Cæcilium.*

His hand into his pocket slipt,
And thence brought forth a manuscript.
He stroked his chin and eke his head,
And thus oracularly read:
"My friends, I ask what brings you hither,
Remember we are met together
To guard the Union, peace, and health,
Of this our glorious commonwealth—
The happiest, you will all agree,
That was, or is, or e'er shall be.
An act has passed our legislature,
Well suited, in its every feature,
To put down gambling, duellings,
Brawls, abolition, pugil rings;
But more than all, said Abolition,
Which means disruption and sedition.

VII.

Hear it, ye Buckeyes! Old-School Quakers!
Ye Hoosiers, Wolverines, and Shakers,
If living still among appeachers—
Hear it, he would have said, ye Beechers!
Ye missionary rifle preachers;
Hear it ye squatters now in Kansas,
From Pasmaquoddy to Aransas;
Hear Chase and Sumner, Seward and Greeley,
And thou most philosophic Silli-
Man, who with Lane, and Brown, and Reeder,
Would'st be regarded a ringleader
Of those unwilling to extend
Slave chattels to our country's end.
Let hear that arch-fanatic Cheever,
Who thirsts as in a raging fever,

Till in his sermon or his prayer,
He thrills the organs of the fair,
And vents unmitigated wrath
On every Southern planter's path;
With fitting words at his command,
To paint this curse upon our land,
And him, that foe to slavery,
Whose *nom de plume* is S. H. T.—
Strange! that a man so prone to ire,
Should glow with vehement desire,
As fame reports, to spread the truth
From east to west, from north to south,
Where'er the ministers of grace
Can preach salvation to our race,
'Till the whole earth with piety
Be filled, as waters fill the sea;
But when the law of Christian love
Can make a tiger as a dove,
Then well may tinkling cymbals sound
Like heavenly strains, o'er hallowed ground.

VIII.

Hear abolition-raving Smith,
Of this conspiracy the pith,
The nerve, the sinew, and the bone,
Thy money-offerings alone
Have in our strongholds made more breaches,
Than all their orators and speeches,
Not even excepting God-send Parker,*
Or Garrison, his brother barker.
Or Thompson's fascinating tongue,†

---

* Theodore.
† George Thompson, of London, or the Rev. J. P. Thompson, New York.

CHIVALRY AND SLAVERY.

Or subtle Campbell's ding-a-dong,
Jay, Giddings, Tappan, Wilson, all,
In Sumner centered, or in Hall.
When pyramids resolve to dust,
The fame of Smith, by moth or rust
Untouched, shall flourish more and more,
And still to loftier regions soar,
Its immortality to find
Among the best of human kind;
Thinks Rubek, mauger errors known,
To fly as clouds before the sun—
The Sun of Righteousness, whose light
Dispels the shades of moral night
From all like him who live and die
In doing works of charity.
And so think all men at the North,
Who know his purity and worth.
Hear all convicted bands of floutlaws,
Rebels, and rioters, and outlaws,
Men armed against our constitution,
And ripe for any revolution,
Such G—d d—d freedom shrieking fellows
Should hang as high as Haman's gallows.

IX.

So lately swung their Saint, John Brown,
Who hoped to win a martyr's crown
By preaching liberty like Moses,
The *wretch !*—and so our law disposes
Of all those miscreants who try
To rob us of our property.
So now would fare the famous Helper,

Or any abolition yelper
Who dares to sermonise or write
Our happy bond-slaves to incite
To that most foul of all disasters,
Revolt against their virtuous masters.
Were Helper here, no judge or jury
Could save him from our people's fury;
His book and he would, both together,
Perfume the air in tar and feather.
Inaugurating—not delivery
From bonds, but something worse than slavery—
New laws to fetter free opinion
Within the bounds of our dominion;
To hang up every mother's son
Who tells a slave his life's his own,
Or any thing thereto belonging
That's worth or having or prolonging;
Talk of the wisdom of past ages,
Our Wise excels all former sages,
As doth the sun a pitch pine torch,
Or starry heavens a lighted porch;
As *gas* what many men call courage,
Or smoking flummery cold porridge!
Sir, those who say a Child can beat him
In writing letters, *underrate him!*

X.

Nor can we praise withhold from Polk,
Keitt, Chestnut, Cobb, and other folk,
Who preach sedition and secession,
In virtue of the foul aggression
On slavery by Northern States,

Whose laws admit of free debates
Upon our slavery constitution:
In short, our every institution,
Instead of hanging up as traitors,
That miscreant crew of agitators,
Who rant such billingsgate and nonsense,
On rights and liberty of conscience."
Thus would the judge have sung or said,
To those who now for negroes plead,
But fame, we think, reports him dead.
All this supposed, *par parenthese*,
We to his Honor's speech retrace
Our steps, to give the peroration
Of his immortal objurgation:
" The law explicitly decrees
To punish these iniquities;
Now if these things by any chance
Should come within your cognizance,
As I well know you're men of wit,
You'll act as you *yourselves* think fit!

DEPORTMENT.

Thus having said, he placed on chair
His coat—his feet he poised in air;
Then spat, and looked august complaisance,
As who should say, " *Revere my presence.*"
Now from the prison to the hall
Of Justice came a criminal,
Who, having ta'en his proper stand,
Was ordered to hold up his hand:
" You *air*," exclaimed the clerk, " indicted,

And *air* before this body cited,
To answer in a serious cause,
A breach upon our buckskin laws.
You cursed and swore most solemnly
That every nigger should go free.
The reason's obvious, and well known,
'Cause you ha'nt any of your own;
For if you had, I know full well,
You'd sooner see them all in hell.
'Tis almost grog-time, so I pray,
Ha'nt you got nothing for to say?"
Enters the witness next: a mope,
For shortness known as C. N. Pope,
He kissed the book, and said "I tell yer,
This scoundrel *Smith*, this same here feller,
Did curse, and swear, and blast, and sink
Himself, if he an easy wink
Would sleep, till black and white should be
Both blessed alike with liberty.
I give you now this evidence,
Appealing to your better sense."

XI.

Up rose a bag of learned bones,
A good blunt man, yclept Squire Jones!
He wiped his mouth with sleeve of coat,
And hem'd, and coughed, and cleared his throat.
" My fellow citizens all round,"
He cried: " I am in duty bound,
As no one else will take my place,
To say a word in this *here* case.
This man said all were equally
Children of Heaven and liberty.

Now, though you his opinion censure,
I to repeat the same adventure.
Should we, who *words* of liberty
Trumpet *abroad* by *land* and *sea*,
At *home* against the *thing* exclaim?
Americans, oh fie! for shame!"
He said no more, but sat him down,
And left them all to stare and frown.

XII.

Silence being ordered by the crier,
Starts up in wrath one M–r–s–ll P'r–y–r;
He placed his hands upon his hips,
And twitched his nose, and bit his lips,
And quickly curved his middle digit,
To scoop a large tobacco pledgitt
From out the hollow of his cheek,
Then hem'd, and thus essayed to speak:
"May I with bowie knives be gnarled—
Although I hate the *barbarous* things,
As serpent bites, or scorpion stings,
Or *Bennet squibs*, or *Potter plugs*,
Or *Lander Pills*, 'atrocious' drugs!—
And into —— for ever har!ed,
If this here business ain't too bad!
By George! 'twill make our niggers mad.
I ask your pardon, sir, for swearing,
Your Honor knows 'tis hard forbearing.
What! let the niggers all go free;
I'll be G—d d——d if that shall be!
Think you what would become of *me*,
Of you, and every man around?
Pray, in God's name, who'd till the ground?

Though I ha'nt got a single acre,
Yet, by the blessing of my Maker,
You know right well my sole dependence
Is on my fellows' strict attendance;
Or those who hire them. With mosquitoes
And gnats all ready for to eat us,
'Twould be a cause of endless strife
Not to have one to fan my wife.
So help me! I'd as soon be hung
As raise the clatter of her tongue;
Though she, in point of *pedigree*,
Ranks first of all who claim to be
F. F.'s in old Virginia;
Lineally come, by marriage laws,
From Pocahontas, *Queen of Squaws!*"

XIII.

Thus he: the crowd with exultation,
And the most vehement laudation,
Express to him their gratulation.
The Judge, with wonted eloquence,
Next sums up all the evidence—
Repeats the statutes of Virginia
Relating to the sons of Guinea;
Then, with well practised knavery,
Quotes scripture text *pro-slavery*.
"We need but glance at, once for all,"
Quoth he, "an argument from Paul:
Was not *Onesimus* a slave?
And did not the apostle crave
His friend Philemon to receive
That base deserter, and forgive
The wrong he did: his debts' amount

Set down in full to Paul's account."
This said, the Judge most plainly shows
That Christianity allows
Of having slaves, and sending back
A fugitive upon his track.
The plot now thickens, and we come
To scenes within the jury-room;
Some vote to set the prisoner free,
And some to hang him on a tree;
Our populace, who seldom falter,
Enter the prison with a halter.
They tie his hands, they shave his head—
Shave all his whiskers and his beard—
(A thing, perhaps, before unheard);
They scourge him till he seems half dead,
They strip him to the skin and bone,
Put tar and feathers thickly on;
The fondest mother scarce would own
In such a coat a darling son.
Like Plato's cock, he looked so queer,
They said he'd make a bishop *leer*.
They send him forth with shouts of laughter,
And pious hopes that he, thereafter,
May mend his manners, nor be free
To prate of human liberty,
At least without regard to color.
Or view to the almighty dollar.

XIV.

Hail Bledsoe! great in mathematics,
Nor less renowned in moral statics;

You prove, in this your wondrous work,
Montesquieu, Blackstone, Locke, and Burke,
On human rights, a squad of boobies,
And equaled only by those loobies,
Hall, Whewell, Paley, Parker, Channing,
And other abolition planning
Quacks who, with Sumner at their head,
And by fanatic notions led,
Would arm the North against the South,
And peril liberty and truth.
Though deemed as men of erudition,
They cannot give a definition
Of liberty or human right.
They err, like all who shun the light.
Those, and those only, you allege,
Can know those rights who would abridge
All right to freedmen but their own,
To furious despotism grown.
In short, those only who have slaves
Can mark the bounds of freedom's waves.
Thy fallacies of abolition
Are matchless, sir ; a recognition
Of that indomitable force
Which signalizes freedom's course.
They prove thee less a subtle critic,
Profoundly skilled in analytic,
Than a poor partisan, whose spite
Is imaged by a midge's bite.

XV.

"Masters claim not to own the soul,
They only exercise control

Upon the *persons* of their slaves,"
Thou sayest! Sir! who the *person rules*
With sovereign sway, *so say* the *schools*,
Has *soul* and *body* for his *tools*.
We've heard thy arguments from knaves,
Who, with the *body in possession*,
Made it a point of free confession
When *serious*, that to *force* the *will*
To the *commission* of such *ill*
As *they desire*, they *cannot fail*
By *power* and *license* to *prevail*.
Slave owners, *self-styled* men high toned,
Are not for self control renowned.
Brooks is an instance, to our mind,
As good as any we can find.
Let who our postulate pretends
To doubt, look round on Southern friends.
Such is the truth, and such must be
One bitter fruit of slavery.
From Exod. it indeed appears,*
That slaves had holes in both their ears;
At least in one, if not in both,
Which ear, however, 'tis in truth
Not very easy to decide,
Nor of importance—specified.
But say that Abraham or† Moses
Had slaves whose ear-holes and their noses
Were large of caliber as hawses,

---

* Exodus xxi. 6. Deut. xv. 17.

† "It might be inferred from the confidence and evident delight with which the example of Abraham is urged in vindication of 'our domestic institution,' that the father of the faithful was also the father of all who traffic in human flesh. If he was, indeed, a slaveholder, he was very far from being the type of a Southern planter. While childless, he designated one of his slaves as his future heir. He was afterwards prevented only by Divine appointment from making the son of the

> For 'tis a savage heritage,
> The right to bore that cartilage,
> And eke with rings and plumes bedight,
> All negroes are *secundum Keitt*
> But *savages,* as in despite
> Of workshops, parlors, gardens, fields,
> And all that civic freedom yields.
> And grant, besides their women slaves,
> To Jews, plurality of wives,

bondwoman heir with the son by promise, and was consoled by the assurance that the former should become the father of princes, and the founder of a great nation. He, moreover, intrusted to one of his slaves the election of a wife for his favorite son.

"The three hundred and eighteen servants born in his house, the Bishop of Texas asserts, were slaves. Still they were men whom he armed and led to battle. They, with their parents, brothers, sisters, wives, and children, must have formed a gang of about two thousand in number. Yet we find the master of this multitude of slaves leaving his guests to catch a calf, to provide dinner for them, while the mistress of the goodly household occupied herself in kneading and baking cakes for her company. A pro-slavery theory alone can blind one to the evidence afforded by these facts, that Abraham was the chief of a clan or tribe, and that the expression 'born in his own house' only indicates that the three hundred and eighteen were not strangers whom he employed on the occasion, but members of the community acknowledging him as its head."—*Introduction by an American clergyman to a reproof of the American Church by the Bishop of Oxford.*

That this servitude (that among the Hebrews) was not founded on the idea of property, appears from the prohibition, "Thou shalt not deliver unto his master the servant which is escaped from his master to thee."—Deut. xxiii. 15.

This law, whether the fugitive were a Jew or heathen, is utterly irreconcilable with common honesty—supposing the servant to have been a mere chattel—and certainly belonged to a very different code of morals from that which enjoins, "If thou meet thy enemy's ox or his ass going astray, thou shalt surely bring it back again to him."—*Ibid.*, 26.

Is slavery or servitude among the Hebrews (supposing, for argument's sake, not admitting, the worst view of the case) more designed as an example or a precept to Christians, by the Divine author of their religion, than the command given to the people of God to destroy the men, women, and children of Canaan? This example, Mr. Bledsoe and his friends will not, it is to be hoped, without a new

CHIVALRY AND SLAVERY.

> Who thence would slavery now defend,
> If they to reason would pretend.
> As Turks or Mormons must, per force,
> Polygamy, the fertile source
> Of countless ills, defend, approve;
> Or else as Christians 'twill behove
> Them all such customs to reject,
> As now unworthy of respect;

and clear and special revelation, advise us to follow in our wars with the Indians. Yet he seems to think the old revelation quite sufficient in the matter of negro slavery. Why it should be so in one case, but not in the other, is, we confess, entirely beyond our comprehension, except upon the new-light theory of the La Grange Convention men, that negro slavery is the greatest missionary enterprise the world ever saw.

Verily, Messrs. Keitt, Gragerty, Womack & Co., ye are bright and shining luminaries upon those dark places of the earth which are full of the habitations of cruelty. You have in your gospel a newer still than the new commandment, that ye love one another; namely, that ye reduce to bondage the whole negro population of Africa: a command which has escaped the sagacity of all the conclaves, synods, and councils of the Christian Church, in all countries, in all ages of its existence.

Ye doctors, confessors, teachers, preachers, and evangelists of the elder dispensation! glorious company of apostles! goodly fellowship of prophets! noble army of martyrs! hide your diminished heads at the approach of those far greater luminaries, the greatest missionaries the world ever saw of the new and divine dispensation.

Go on, gentlemen! A few more conventions like those of Charleston, Savannah, and La Grange; a few more *pronunciamentos*, like that of a late Governor of South Carolina; a few more Louisville and Baltimore massacres; a few more filibustering expeditions; a little more overwrought zeal and rampant patriotism of the wise men of Virginia, will do more to run the thing of slavery into the ground than all the great efforts of all the great leaders of abolition in Congress.

There are, fortunately, in the Slave States thousands of planters and others, as much opposed as any Abolitionist can be to the views of Governor Alston, of South Carolina, and his convention friends, Womack & Co., upon the revival of the African slave trade; thousands who do not, cannot think the preceding language too severe against men entertaining such preposterous, such abominable notions.

Conflicting with their constitutions,
Their laws, and other institutions;
Their manners, habits, rites, and creeds;
Their peace, their interests, and needs.
Those things were for a time allowed,
While yet the chosen tribes were rude;
For circumstances alter cases
In individuals as in masses.
Now that the Gospel's glorious light
Has scattered ignorance and night,
The hardness of the heart of man
A cause sufficient never can
Be deemed, or for polygamy,
Divorce, or human slavery.
But rude as men were under Moses,
His slave laws this great truth discloses,
That slaves were *then* much better used,
And much less beaten, worked, and bruised,
Than they are now, as may be shown
By very brief comparison
Of every Slave State statute-book,
And those found in the Pentateuch.
What master sets his bond slave free
If he smites out his tooth or eye?*
Who advocates a jubilee,
Which would to all bring liberty?
A female slave, as wife or daughter,
Was not to fetch or wood or water,
Like Helots; or go out as men.
Her food, her raiment, and her pin

---

* If a man smite the eye of his servant or the eye of his maid, that it perish, he shall let him go free for his eye's sake. And if he smite out his man servant's tooth, or his maid servant's tooth, he shall let him go free for his tooth's sake. —Exodus xxi. 26, 27.

CHIVALRY AND SLAVERY.

Allowance paid ; or, failing these*
Conditions, she all penalties
Of bondage might thereafter 'scape,
And, as she pleased, work, wed, or trape
Some model Jefferson, good Bledsoe,†
No doubt might treat a favorite slave so :

---

* And if a man sell his daughter to be a maid servant she shall not go out as the men servants do. If she please not her master who hath betrothed her to himhimself, then shall he let her be redeemed.

And if he hath betrothed her to his son, he shall deal with her after the manner of daughters. If he take him another wife, her food, her raiment, and her duty of marriage, shall not diminish. And if he do not these three things unto her, then shall she go out free without money.—Exodus xxi., 7-11.

† This gentleman, in his most pretentious treatise on pro-slavery dialectics, lauds and magnifies himself in imaginary victories over Locke, Paley, Channing, Montesquieu, Macaulay, and others. Yet there is not in the whole of his humdrum argumentation a single paragraph that is novel, interesting, instructive, or amusing. His arguments, so called, against those eminent writers, are alike disingenuous and flimsy. All that need be said of him and others of the same school is, that they get their living, or have been born in Slave States; that they are like that man of Ephesus, so wise in his generation, who, perceiving that his craft was in danger by the introduction of Christianity, became tenfold more vehement than ever in his zeal for the honor and worship of his goddess. Those gentlemen, to say the least, and secluding the worst possible cause, act in one particular with singular indiscretion, provoking a controversy with writers, who are both in number and talents immeasurably their superiors.

Some of them, it is true, write books and sell them. If they succeed in that censorship of the press to which they are now invited, with a bishop at their head, viz., by preparing such a series of books in every department of study, from the earliest primer to the highest grade of literature and science (no query as to their competency), as shall seem to them best qualified (*sic*) to elevate and purify the education of the South! and, thereby, of course, to perpetuate slavery, they will have attained the acme of all their worldly ambition; and, as we have already proved, or hope more abundantly to prove, in these simple rhymes, have added, (can they think so?) to their faith, virtue; and to virtue, knowledge; and to knowledge, temperance; and to temperance, patience; and to patience, godliness; and to godliness, brotherly kindness; and to brotherly kindness, charity—that charity which prompts us to do unto others as we would that they should do unto us.

CHIVALRY AND SLAVERY.

One *who*, no antitype of *Bozes*,
All women equal presupposes.

If science, as well as literature and religion, become abolitionist, as no doubt she will (nay, ever has been), we well may commiserate their attempts to reform her. We had, in our ignorance, imagined that even a proscription of obscene books was already impossible. But what can be impossible with men who, in these days of railroads and steamboats, can suppress the circulation of many of the very best in our language! Pride's purge, gentlemen! was a strong purge, but weak in comparison with the purge of your folly. Some of you, clergymen and lawyers, have been considered so liberal, on diversity of opinion, in religion and politics, that you were supposed to be the bitterest enemies of the *Index Expurgatorius* of Rome! But, is there, or is there not to be an *Index Expurgatorius* of Charleston, Savannah, or New Orleans? Alas! gentlemen, must the works of Hall, Cowper, Willberforce, and Channing, be cast to the moles and to the bats, and the illustrated obscenities of cards, novels, and model statuary, be the order of the day? The time was, when you all freely admitted that slavery is an evil—a great evil, a deadly evil—which you lamented, but could not at present get rid of, yet hoped to see ultimately removed; you have lately changed ground and regard it as a blessing; yea, even as a divine institution—"the greatest of all missionary enterprises!"

Which of these views shall we adopt—the present view or the past?

But slavery and slaveowners must be let alone! Indeed! But was it so from the beginning? Did Moses let Pharaoh alone and the other breeders, speculators, taskmasters, and oppressors of Hebrew bondmen in Egypt? Did Christ let the Pharisees alone; or the Apostles acquiesce in the corruptions of Paganism? Did Luther let alone Indulgences, or the preachers and abettors of the doctrine of Indulgences? The fact is, there can be no compromise between truth and error, light and darkness, Christ and Belial! The conflict is irrepressible.

We, you assert, have no mission in this matter. Every one has a mission, in a good sense, to impart, according to his measure, the light that is in him. You, gentlemen, in common with ourselves, have lately had, still have, some share in a mission against those pests to society, the Mormons; not reflecting, possibly, that Mormonism and Slavery agree in one; that there is, in fact, as there must be, in Slave States, as much Mormonism in certain relations of life, as ever existed in Turkey or Utah.

Our slaveholders of the South, many of them prime movers, nay, constituting with their abettors and tools the aggregate of the pious fraternity of filibusters, claim a mission peculiar, extraordinary, and divine—a mission of which Walker is, or was, the head—a mission of manifest destiny, *i. e.*, manifest cupidity, against

CANTO VI.

Planters, overseers, and traffickers in human flesh, commonly called negro-traders, or speculators, compared, contrasted, &c. Two recent murders, selected from thousands, show how this home-traffic works. First case, that of Sambo, a slave. Second, that of Prince, respectively described. Overseers turned planters. Their brutality and cruelty, generally speaking. A benevolent planter. Dialogue between Messrs. Jones and Smith, in reference to Brown's crop of sugar. Robinson, Jones' overseer. His system of labor. Losses. Murder of Robinson. Unprofitableness of excessive labor, and severity. Squire Jones' wise resolution.

I.

While some among our Southern planters
Intolerant are as covenanters,
And low and boisterous as ranters,

their fellow-republicans of Central America: not for the extension of the principles of free government, which those people already possess, or do not desire at such hands, but avowedly for the preservation of the balance of power by the Southern States of this Union, and the establishment, diffusion, and perpetuity of slavery. They have also a mission of manifest destiny against the island and government of Cuba, and all its institutions and laws. It embraces even the whole Continent of America, and all the islands of the Ocean; nay, more, it is the one great mission superseding all others, the mission of slavery: whose apostles—the apostles of slavery—are commissioned to go into the whole world and preach their gospel to every creature.

Verily, it comes with a bad grace from the slaveholders of the South, to twit their fellow-citizens with impertinent intermeddling in slavery; as if the institutions of a common country were none of their business; while they, themselves (the slaveholders), are perpetually meddling with a foreign sovereign people of another race, with whom their country is at peace, and who are far beyond the sphere of their legitimate intervention.

But slavery is one of our institutions. Admitted. Institutions, evil in their very nature, ought, like other evils, be abolished by those who have a right, whose duty it is to abolish them. Paganism, Buddhism, Mahometanism, are, with their multiform abominations, all institutions. Monarchy was once in these United States an institution, universally recognized. Auguries, Lupercalia, Flamines, Corybantes, Epulones, amphitheatres, idols, sacrificial rites and ceremonies,

Others, as numerous there be,
True models of civility.
Between the good and very bad,
In short, is every hue and shade;
The speculator, or overseer,
Part fox, part tiger, and part bear,
Part hog, part monkey, and part wolf, is
A wide, impenetrable gulf, is
Betwixt the one class and the other.
The planter, never as a brother,
A friend, an equal, or a neighbor,
But as a needful tool of labor,
Views the o'erseer or speculator,*

---

were, together with that very hydra, slavery—against which we are contending—all institutions of Rome.

Those who are not completely Gibbonized—under the influence, that is, of the anti-Christian anodynes of that prince of scoffers, the author of "The Decline and Fall of the Roman Empire"—will admit the wrath, riot, and confusion, which took place throughout the Roman world, when those institutions, associated and interwoven with the inmost frame and constitution of their civil polity, their statutes, ordinances, and regulations—the education, the prejudices, the superstitions, the habits, manners, and customs—the passions, enjoyments, and interests of priests and people—gave way, before the preaching of the Gospel, like a mist before the rays of a tropical sun; or, as in the vision of the King of Babylon, the images of clay, iron, brass, and gold, crumbled and were broken into pieces by that stone cut out without hands, which became a great mountain, and filled the whole earth.

Slavery, gentlemen, cannot stand, and you know it; and, to use the words of a great political reformer, we know that you know it, and you know that we know that you know it. Hence it is you are so nervous, irritable, and zealous, at our naming it. Hence it is you so often say, "Talk to us no more on this subject;" but, we will talk, nevertheless, gentlemen, though our testimony, like that of the noble Sumner, should be sealed with our blood.

* It is unnecessary, on this side the Atlantic, to show the general estimation in which slave-traders are held. One or two authorities may suffice to convince us in what light they are regarded by thinking men in Europe:—

"When we come down to Christianity," said the Bishop of St. David's, in the

CHIVALRY AND SLAVERY.

As *sui generis*, a creature,
Through whom he tries, tho' oft in vain,
Wealth, power, and station to obtain.
But negro-traders and o'erseers,
Are most harmonious compeers
In *unity-duality*,
In both, compound equality,
In all things, base rascality.
Brutal, unprincipled, ferocious,
They stop at nothing, how atrocious
Soever it may chance to be;
However stained with cruelty,
If it puts money in their pocket,
No matter if it shame the docket
In infamy, provided proof
Be wanting, to keep fear aloof
Of law or punishment, or both;
For law receives no negro's oath
Against a white man, if his will
Should be a dozen slaves to kill,
Supposing that no white man saw
The deed committed—such the law—
The murderer would be acquitted,
And all the penalty remitted.
One near us whispers the suggestion
Of a remission out of question:

House of Lords (1606), "we find that dealers in slaves are held among the worst of the human race." St. Paul, in his Epistle to Timothy, tells what the dealers in slaves are, and who are their companions. The slave-dealers are called stealers of men and their companions are liars, perjurers, murderers, and parricides.

Bishop Horsely (1799), after proving that the men-stealers, classed in the Bible with murderers of fathers and murderers of mothers, were in fact, according to the true meaning of the Greek word, slave-traders, adds, "We have reason to conclude from the mention of slave-traders by St. Paul, that if any of them should find their way to heaven, they must go thither in company with murderers and parricides."

When charges are not entertained,
'Tis as if nobody complained.

II.

Two recent murders, in our view,
Prove what we say, alas! too true—
Murders by blood negotiators,
In courtesy called speculators—
Slaves might well name them separators,
Because it seems their scheme of life,
Parents and children, man and wife,
To part, and break, in human ties,
Consanguineal sympathies.
We knew these fellows but too well;
The one named Cobb, the other Creel.
The varlets purchased two *men's lives;*
Those men, like *other men,* had wives,
And children too; and both objected
To go to Texas. They reflected
That they might just as well be dead
As by such vampires captive led,
And into cruel bondage sold,
Where they could ne'er again behold
Wives, children, parents, homes, or friends:
Where hope in desolation ends.
Sambo in irons was secured,
His safe delivery insured;
But from his cruel owners broke
So soon as he could slip his yoke.
He then his footsteps 'gan retrace,
To see his wife's abiding place.
The sum of just two hundred dollars,
Without account of caste or colors,
To captors, as a meet reward,
Was offered in poor Sam's regard—

Alive or dead. An Indian who
Poor Sam's retreat was wont to know,
To save the trouble of departure
From home, made sure his victim's capture
By simply blowing out his brains,
And sending for the proffered gains.

III.

We saw poor Sam! He lived three days
In stupor or in wild amaze;
His brains bedropping down his face,
Blinded his eyes. He could not see,
Nor hear, nor taste, apparently;
Nor did he speak, or once complain
Of all his sorrow or his pain,
But looked unutterable woes
On all around, or friends or foes.

IV.

We learn that Prince has just expired;
Of life and lingering torments tired.
Since first the rifle's fatal track,
Some three days since, had ploughed his back,
He lived in agony; yet glad
To think his death, however sad,
Would rid him of a life of pain
And wretchedness, for others' gain.
His only crime was that he ran,
Or so attempted, from a man
Whom to behold is but to hate
Worse than a rattlesnake or rat.
A most perfidious sort of villain;
A thief, a swindler, a rampallian.
Now wives and children sore lament,
These murders rash and truculent.

Yet as poor negroes are but chattels,
Who talks of punishment but twattles;
There never would be wanting elves
To swear that they had killed themselves;
Perhaps *were* killed in self defence,
Secluding malice called prepense,
By men whose lives they had attainted,
And would have slain, if not prevented.

v.

From Prince, the *latest information*
States that his constant supplication
Was of his days a prolongation,
Till he could better be prepared,
In faith, to hope for the reward
Which he, perhaps, too slightly prized,
Or had to passion sacrificed.
That he most bitterly complained
Of his foul murderer, and arraigned
Him constantly before the bar
Where murdered and the murderer
Must both on trial soon appear;
That he lamented the estate
Of all like *him*, whose hapless fate
Is thus interminably hung
Or from the arm or from the tongue
Of ruthless and capricious tyrants,
Without or law's or reason's warrants;
That he had nothing left in life,
Except his children and his wife,
From which he parted with regret:
He left for them an amulet,
By which who wore it was secure,
In way of antidote or cure,

Against the bite of rattlesnakes.
Alas! poor Prince! it something takes
More potent than thy simple charm
To keep thy family from harm;
Those worse than serpents to disarm,
Who thus have cruelly decreed
Thy doom, and may cause them to bleed,
If anger should the love of treasure
In savage hearts like theirs outmeasure.
Adieu! poor Prince! thy foes forgive,
The Saviour died that thou might'st live.

VI.

When overseers are turned planters,
And fond of bottles and decanters,
Then more than commonly irate,
It is impossible to state
The aggregate of crime and wrong
They perpetrate their slaves among.
They cannot rise to the same station
Of dignity and elevation
Which men, perhaps, of wealth inferior,
But of acquirements far superior,
Attain; as must be in those States
Where worth, not wealth, respect awaits.
Low and unprincipled, and base,
They cannot reach the lowest place
Where only gentlemen are met,
On public matters to debate;
Or in those social circles sit,
For which they feel they are unfit.
But then at home, where none dispute
Their power, they show the human brute.
See such a man, a slave his victim,
No law or jury to convict him,

You cannot, in his wrath, depict him.
One may, of course, exceptions trace,
In this, as almost every case.
One sometimes finds an overseer,
To whom our censures can't refer,
But speculators, every one,
Come under our proscription ban.

VII.

Planters who are of high repute,
Humane, benevolent, and kind,
Courteous, upright, and honorable,
Truthful, reliable, and stable,
Think, being such, they can refute
All anti-slavery men, and find
In their own hearts, an answer suited
To all the questions ever mooted—
To prove that slavery far worse is
Than all the other deadly curses,
Since Cain first saw his hands imbrued
With the red tide of Abel's blood.
Those planters err, the very best,
The ills of slavery attest,
They often prove the instruments,
And see the dreadful increments
Of crime, derived from their demeanor,
And very gentleness of manner.

VIII.

Quoth Jones to Smith, "I saw in town
My friend and neighbor, Aaron Brown—
He tells me that, with eighty hands,
He makes of cane, in upper lands,
One thousand hogsheads of fine sugar.
He must in truth be a hard tugger,

I cannot, with an equal number,
Perfect machinery, and lumber,
Much more than half that *quantum* make.
There's Day and Martin, Doyle and Hunter,
And, what's his name? that hoary grunter,
Mac, something, living on our coast—
Whose slave, from fearing something worse,
Jumped with his chain into the river,
They have not yet fished up his corse,
Nor will they, I imagine, ever,—
Who, in my hearing, often boast,
That with my slaves they'd undertake
To raise three hundred more than Brown.
They oven swear it down and down,
And that with full one hundred firkins
Of *syrop* more than Scamp or Jerkins."
"By what Freemasonry," says Smith,
"For unto me it seems a myth?"
"Why, simply this," replied his friend,
" By extra working of his slaves.
A man, who every danger braves,
Of fire and dagger, axe and poison,
May every day increase his foison;
But I can see no potent reason,
My fortunes by such means to mend."

IX.

Now, Robinson, the overseer,
Who happened to be standing near,
Promptly rejoined, "I'll tell you what, sir!
You never can, no, you can *not*, sir,
Compete with any planting neighbor—
You interfere so with our labor.
If you to me the matter leave,
And all your toil and trouble save,

I'll venture boldly to insure you,
That is, provided I can cure you
Of what, I said before, both vain is
And of our industry the bane is,
I shall not hurt a single hand
By double produce of your land."
"Well, Robinson, at least, I'll try you,
And promise not to mortify you,"
Quoth good Squire Jones, "by any order
Which your prerogatives may border.
I wish your labor duly rated,
But still would have my slaves well treated."

X.

Two hours before the daylight shone,
They worked as horses, every one;
Nor young nor old, nor big nor little,
Found rest, but during sleep or victual;
Nor ceased till daylight disappeared,
And they the screech-owl's voice had heard.
No prayers, no Sabbath day for them;
No song, no dance, no solemn hymn;
While *sugar-grinding* all the night,
They, in relays, were worked, till light
Again proclaimed continuous work,
Hunger and thirst, and rancid pork.
That year the sugar-house was burned,
All plans, all hopes were overturned,
All pledges were made null and void,
And present profits quite destroyed;
Death took at least a score of slaves,
O'ertasked, o'erworked, unjustly whipped,
They sank to their untimely graves;
All prospects in the bud were nipped,

CHIVALRY AND SLAVERY.

And Robinson, who daily ordered
Some wrongful chastisement, was murdered.
Two slaves were for the murder tried,
Condemned, and hanged, but they denied
All guilt, and, unrepenting, died,
With blood and vengeance satisfied.

XI.

Squire Jones, who, as we should have stated,
Was absent a whole year, now dated
All his misfortunes to the vigor,
The ceaseless, cruel, brutal rigor,
To which, to rival Day and Martin,
Scamp, Jerkins, Hunter, Doyle, McAlpin,
Themselves the victims to their graves
Of secret plots among their slaves,
His overseer had so resorted,
As we have faithfully reported,
Now, evermore resolved to see
The exercise of clemency,
And, with more profit and less labor,
Show good example to his neighbor.

CANTO VII.

The old Judge and his book. His views of Slavery. Curse of Ham. Designs of Providence. Benefit of Slavery to Africa. Conversion to Christianity. European Missionaries. Comparative failure of. Negro Missionaries. African tribes in a state of perpetual warfare. Cannibalism. Future African Bishoprics. Diocesan divisions. Restoration of Africans and Jews. The Fable again, Facial Angles. Amalgamation. Cyprian. Augustine. Bishops Elliott and Heber.

I.

A certain judge, aged eighty-four,
'Twas said, we thought him ten years more,

Supposing B. had studied Greek,
And with authority could speak,
Ere he (the judge) wished death to brave,
Would know if δουλος* meant a slave,

* Slaves, as long as they were under the government of masters, were called οικεται, but after their freedom was granted them, they were δουλοι, not being, like the former, a part of their master's estate, but only obliged to some grateful acknowledgments and small services, such as were required of Μετοικοι, to whom they were in some few things inferior.—*Potter's Antiquities of Greece,* c. ʌ., p. 59.

If the present generation of slaveholders had lived under the government of Greece, in the days of Pericles—or of Rome, in those of Domitian, when Lydians, Syrians, Paphlagonians, Gauls, Britons, and Dacians were slaves—they would find the same arguments in favor of the system which they now use in defence of African slavery; namely, the moral, physical, and intellectual inferiority of the races enslaved, adding, if Christians or Hebrews, the authority of the Bible, and the curse of Ham! Allow the poor African in these days (facial angles, notwithstanding) the same opportunities and advantages of education as some slaves enjoyed in those, they would, doubtless, soon rise above the level of their present condition, and exhibit to the admiration of contemporaries and of posterity—not perhaps for many generations, if ever, the faultless figure of many an aboriginal Indian, or, the more acute facial angle, the refined physiognomical contour and symmetrical proportions of an aristocratic European—but, what is still better, such literary pre-eminence as that of those illustrious bondsmen, Esop, Terence, and Epictetus. The genius of Dumas is not the less brilliant, that its light is derived in a great measure from an African origin.

"Is it certain that bondsmen, so called by our translators, but not distinguished in the original Scriptures from servants, were slaves?" The word in the original, sometimes rendered bondsman, sometimes servant, is *Obed.* It is applied to Christ: Behold my servant, whom I uphold! It is applied to King Rehoboam: I. Kings xii. 7. Ziba, Saul's Obed, had himself twenty Obeds: II. Samuel ix. 10. We find, I Chronicles ii. 34, that Sheshai, the head of one of the families of the tribe of Judah, gave his daughter and wife to his servant, an Egyptian; and so far was any disgrace, in consequence, from being attached to their children, that the son of this very daughter was enrolled among the valiant men of David's army: I. Chron. ii. 41.—*See Reproof, &c.,* p. 21.

That servants are in some few instances in Scripture called the money of their masters may signify nothing more than they were the means of their living. Mechanics, journeymen, apprentices, farm laborers, and others, may certainly, without overstraining a figure of speech, be called the money of their employers.

CHIVALRY AND SLAVERY.

Such veritable slaves, as we
Pronounce unfit for liberty.
"You know," said he, "I mean our niggers,
Domestics, choppers, reapers, diggers."
He gravely then began to quote
From reams of foolscap, which he wrote,
To prove that Slavery is a blessing,
Beyond most others, worth possessing;
That 'tis man's natural estate
That few men ever can be great;
That they must serve, as is most fit,
Those bless'd with greater power and wit;
That paddles, cowhides, cudgels, thwacks,
Were all designed for nigger backs;
That now to free the race of Cain
Was idle, foolish, devilish, vain.
The curse of Ham is on them all,
Or young or old, or great or small.
He quoted largely from Bible,
To show it was a silly libel
On scripture, slavery to call
In question, as it must befall
A portion of the human race,
Aside from others far less base.

II.

That slaves had holes in both their ears,
From Exod. xxi. appears.
He proved that Providence designed
Thus to instruct the negro mind;
That He, with whom a thousand years
Are as a day, His mode prefers
To ours, whose structures, wrought of clay,
As airy visions fade away.

'Twas thus the Hebrews under Pharaoh,
And thus the Christians under Nero,
Baptized in sufferings, were trained,
And thus for glory disciplined.
If, of the race, a generation,
Or five or ten, by transportation
From Afric's coast, were all made slaves,
Who, but your abolition knaves,
Would look upon it as a price
Too high, too great a sacrifice,
If they with Christian truth imbued,
And Christian virtues were endued?

III.

"How great the company of preachers,"
Said B., " when slaves become the teachers
Of those in Africa, who now
To heathen idols vainly bow.
Their education soon would fit them,
Should we instruct and manumit them,
To be apostles of a clime
Where, or inland, or maritime,
Our missionary labors fail,
Or seldom are of much avail,
That sable race to Christianize,
And our fond wishes realize.
Witness our efforts in Goree,
Medina, Bathurst, and La Bee,
Or Guinea, or Sierra Leone,
Or Benin, or that apogeon
Of missionary light, Beroo,
Käarta, Jenné, Tombuctoo.
If, in Liberia, more success
Our Christianizing efforts bless,

CHIVALRY AND SLAVERY.

We owe it to emancipation,
Wrought by our own colonization.

IV.

Monrovia, Harperstown, and Greenville,
As those who've visited those scenes will
Bear witness, prove that slaves made free
Do more for Christianity
Than all our other Christian teachers,
However excellent as preachers.
There may be some this fact who question,
From ignorance or indigestion,
Then let them prove it false, if they
A visit to Liberia pay.
Denham and Clapperton, the Landers,
And all who Quorra's strange meanders
Have traced, and who can best describe,"
Rejoined the Judge, " each ebon tribe,
With unanimity declare
That they are evermore at war.
They state, moreover, it appears,
That they or kill their prisoners,
Or make them slaves, or have them sold
As slaves, for merchandise or gold,
To traders visiting the coast,
Or eat them parboiled, raw, or roast."
" Not yet the time, but it must come,"
Quoth B., "when slaves returning home,
Across the desert of Sahara,
Shall spread the Gospel through Bambarra,
Dacomba, Yoruba, Mandara,
The gold coast, ivory and grain coast—
Pray, let it not be deemed a vain boast—
From Harperstown to Ashantee,
Will, centering at Coomassie,

With Cape Coast Castle and Abomey,
Be made thy *Diocese*, Dahomey.

V.

Benin, Biafra, and Loango,
Will make a *second*, joined with Congo,
Close by the Quorra, Tombuctoo,
With Housa, Bigharmi, Bornou,
Extending round thy coast, Lake Tchadd!
To British memories so sad,*
Shall be regarded as *another*
Within thy charge, our sable brother.
Along the west from Delagoa,
Extending northward to Quillóa.
In Zanguebar and Mosambique,
The natives will a fourth bespeak.
Thence to the straits of Babel Mandel,
Thro' Ajan, Sonmali, who *can* tell
What future Moses may conduct them
Back to the lands from which we've plucked them;
Not flying now from slavery,
But independent, great, and free,
Across the channel of that sea,
Where Pharaoh and his chivalry
Before Jehovah's anger fled,
A numerous host lay stark and dead.
Thus travelling onward to their farms,
Their sons and daughters in their arms,
On camels' backs and dromedaries,
In transits, called *hebdomedaries*,
Not only with their beasts of burden
Will they obtain some pleasant Jordan,

---

* See Lander's Travels.

Our steamers and our railroad cars
Will furnish all particulars,
Which are to wayfarers essential,
For all is clearly Providential."

VI.

Not less of Africans than Jews,
Thus prophesies our Christian muse:
"Our chambers, parlors, workshops, fields,"
Remarked the judge, "are helps and shields,
To save them from the precipice
Of want and indolence and vice,
When whole millenniums shall have passed,
In bondage, so supremely blessed
As theirs is now, they needs must be
All, in the Lord Jehovah, free!
Their facial angles less obtuse,
They doubtless will have perfect use
Of tongues, and gifts, and powers of mind,
To aid the weak, to guide the blind.

VII.

" At Alexandria or Cairo,
Or where, immortalized by Maro,
Carthage," quoth B., " defiance hurled
At Rome, the mistress of the world;
Or say at Hippo, or at Läis,
Or Utica, or Ptolemäis,
Or on the Delta of the Nile,
Or straits where Moslem saints defile;
Or where in Sennaar's fertile plain
The graceful Nubian reaps his grain,
And, from the summit of a rock,
Beholds a lion in his flock.

Upon the banks of the Albara,
Or yet at Gondar of Amhara,
In Abyssinia, as of old,
Men may again the cross behold,
With banner to the breeze unfurled,
A badge of triumph to the world.

VIII.

Some sable Cyprian may arise,
Or Athanasius, great and wise,
Or spotless Austin write and teach,
And highest excellency reach;
Or Origen, whose eagle flight
Pierced far beyond the solar light;
Or Chrysostom, whose dauntless tongue
With priceless treasures round him flung,
Was wont his hearers' hearts to hold
As compassed with a chain of gold.
Speed Heaven! the happy times that may
Restore such men to Africa.
About or Cyprian's facial angle,
Or Chrysostom's, 'twere vain to wrangle,
Since both, as Africans, deny
The right to human slavery.

IX.

But say they were not of the race
Which you and Elliott think so base!
Certes, they were thine equals, Elliott!
And each, as thou, a Christian zealot,
Perhaps the angles of their faces
Did not, like thine, *display the Graces!*
Birth, worth, and talents, and high station
Are a most charming combination.

CHIVALRY AND SLAVERY.

With piety and learning crowned,
They claim a homage most profound,
And all contribute to unfold
The aspects of a perfect mould;
Befitting caskets for a mind,
With every gift of Heaven refined.
Such gifts *are* Elliott's, such *were* Heber's,
Beyond the common lot of neighbors.
The difference between them lies
In this, that one would not disguise
His horror of that human bondage
Which t'other thinks but *lawful poundage;*
For slaves come into one's possession
By hereditary succession."*

X.

When B. thus ended his oration,
He left the judge in perturbation,
Then called a very little boy
(The old man's grandson). When he came,

---

* That a rhetorician so fascinating, a gentleman so accomplished and of a personal presence so highly *distingué*, as Bishop Elliott, could find much to say on the subject of slavery—which, to a lady traveller of gentle blood and courtly breeding, like the honorable Miss Murray, would seem altogether unanswerable—will surprise no one, who has any knowledge of the best society of the slave-holding States. Dr. Elliott might have refe.red her, possibly, to the menage of his own household, or to that of many others of his acquaintance, as models of subordination, harmony, and comfort. But let him go to the plantation quarters, have a thorough knowledge of overseers, speculators, and their doings—of field operations, etc., the moral, physical, social, religious, intellectual condition of all around —let the experience of half, or even quarter of a century, have its perfect work in this matter, unbiased by prejudice or interest, uninfluenced by any of those ten thousand considerations which mislead or make captive the understanding; and if any one of sane mind, who chooses to submit or who has submitted to such an ordeal, do not arrive at the same conclusion as that of the author of these poems, touching slavery—he, the author of said poems, will undertake, to the manifest peril of his digestion and life, to eat up the roll of this manuscript.

B. asked him if he were not able
One or two moments to employ,
From Æsop's Greek, to read a fable,
And see that it was well translated.
The Dog and Wolf, B. chose to name,
As to the Georgian he had stated.
The worthy judge the tale heard through,
And, sighing, said to him 'twas new.
He then took up his hat and cane,
And never troubled B. again.
So true it is what Holy Writ,
With vastly more than human wit,
Saith to this point, so oft detected—
"From children's lips is praise perfected."

XI.

It is susceptible of proof,
That persons in the highest station
Have servants, who, for their behoof,
Live in the open violation
Of that great law of moral life,
Touching not only man and wife,
But all to whom such law is given,
By the authority of Heaven.
How hostile to miscegenations
Are white men living on plantations,
And foes to all emancipations,
Let different shades of color own,
From darkest *griffe* to bright *quadroon*.
It may appear a case uncommon,
That son and sire should of one woman
Be both the paramours; but we
Oft find such facts in slavery.
A man, we now and then behold,
Whose sister "is his children's mother."

CHIVALRY AND SLAVERY.

Such unions, and so manifold,
Are found impossible to smother;
They show most clearly in reflection
The various shadings of complexion,
For every lineament and feature
Is drawn with all the skill of nature;
Nor stamp, nor letterpress can be
Proof stronger of paternity.

XII.

Many their children all enslave,
And thus *expense* of *labor save*,
If they in *bondage hold* the *mother ;*
But if in bondage to another,
Her children are her *master's chattels*,
So law determines all such titles.

XIII.

Slave women privileged to hire
Their time, and live as they desire,
By paying certain weekly wages,
Will often be induced to act
In such a manner as, in fact,
Would, if described, defile our pages.
Thus, many live by prostitution,
In virtue of this institution;
Masters and mistresses are made
Sharers in profits of the trade—
Nay, oft depend for all their inning
On this most hopeless sort of sinning;
Nathless are socially thought pure,
And of their standing quite secure,
As members of a Slave State union,
And in some church's full communion,

CHIVALRY AND SLAVERY.

In which such things are tolerated,
And never heard as reprobated:
In short, the thing is far too common
To shock the ears of man or woman
In churches South; yet time shall be,
When all shall curse such infamy.

CANTO VIII.

Roly-polies. Felony to teach them the Alphabet. Parlor and Cabin. Romance of Louisiana! George and Monsieur G. H. D——l. His Terrors and Tyranny. Determination to die rich. "The Death of the Righteous." (Notes on the Hon. Miss Murray and the Bishop of Georgia, Monsieur G. of Louisiana and a certain Western Trader among the Indians.)

I.

KIND ladies talk of "Roly-polies," *
And tell us gallo-taurine stories,
And write the nicest allegories
About our little negro *jolies*.
Some talk of Santa Claus and banjos,
And eke boleros and fandangos,
And some of preachings and convertings
And silly Scriptural pervertings,
Like sorry jests of hard-shell sconces
For Harper's Monthly, sent by dunces;
But not a word of whips and chains,
Ropes, paddles, collars, thwacks and pains.
This sort of talking, on the whole, is
Fudge! and an instance of their follies.
Black little children will be merry,
Crisp, cosy, curly, sleek, and fat,
With skins that shine like a blackberry,

---

* Negro children—so called by the amiable, gifted, and to-be-lamented lady, E. T. Wortley.

CHIVALRY AND SLAVERY.

Especially if greased, and Lady W.
Is with a visit going to trouble you.
But all admitted—what of that?
Save this, that in them human nature
Is sunk, debased in every feature.

II.

That slaves are children all, in mind,
Stupid, untutored, weak, and blind;
That 'tis a felony to teach them
Their A, B, C, lest men should preach them
Into a knowledge of the worth
Of life and freedom, and so forth,
Is one great fact, left out by those
Who fain would lead men by the nose.
To think that they desire such light
As would from slaves dispel the night
Of ignorance, that they might be
In time prepared for liberty.
Can such assertions help a cause,
Which light precludes by penal laws?
Man's mental progress without schools,
Or books, or teachers, is of fools
The theory, if not of knaves,
Determined enemies of slaves.
If knowledge only should make free,
Why make *instruction felony?* *

---

* To teach slaves to read is forbidden, under the severest penalties, in almost every Slave State.

In North Carolina, to teach a slave to read or write, or give him any book (the Bible not excepted), is punished with thirty-nine lashes, or imprisonment, if the offender be a free negro; with a fine of two hundred dollars, if he be a white.

In Georgia, the fine is five hundred dollars; and the father is not suffered to teach his half-caste child to read the Scriptures.—*Reproof,* &c., p. 48.

"At this very moment," says Bishop Elliott, "there are from three to four mil-

But chambers, parlors, workshops, fields,
Transcend for slaves what learning yields.

lions of African slaves, educating for earth and for heaven, in the so vilified Southern States; educating in a thousand ways of which the world knows nothing; educating in our nurseries, in our chambers, in our parlors, in our workshops, and in our fields, as well as in our churches, &c. God's ways are not discordant with the ways of slavery. He (*God!*) cares very little for the present means through which His will is working. What is it that a man should be a slave, if through that means he may become a Christian? What is it that one or even ten generations should be *slaves*, if through that arrangement a race be training for future glory and self-dependence? My feeling just now is, that I would defend it against all interference, just as I should defend my children from any one who would tempt them to an improper independence; just as I should defend any relation of life which man was attempting to break, or to violate, ere the purpose of God in it had been worked out."—*United States, Canada, and Cuba*, pp. 349, 350.

Is it not astonishing that the shrewd intellect of the honorable Miss Murray did not intuitively discern the consequences of the principle that God cares very little for present means; and is it not still more astonishing that Dr. Elliott should himself have published to the world such a sample of Georgian theology!

If it had been enunciated by a Jesuit, the bishop and the lady would, both of them, at a glance have perceived that it is the old fallacy of the end justifying the means—supposing, that is, that slave-pirates, speculators, &c., had ever any other end in view than their own selfish interests in the capture or purchase of slaves!

"God," says the bishop, "cares very little for the present means through which His will is working." Indeed! We had, in our simplicity, always imagined that God cares a *great deal* for the means through which His will is working, else we are guilty of solemn mockery in His sight when we pray, as it is to be presumed we do frequently, in the words which He has Himself taught us, that He would *bless* and *sanctify* those "means" for the advancement of His empire in our hearts and for the accomplishment of *His will* upon *earth* by *mankind, as in heaven* by the *spirits that minister at His throne*.

If *prayers, preaching, sacraments,* &c., be but *means* of rendering to Him the homage due to His divine sovereignty—if He enjoins upon us the duty of *well-doing* as *one* of the *means* of future happiness—if it be our doctrine that while prohibiting He permits evil, and *overrules* it as a *means* for working out His designs—we cannot for a moment submit to those loose theological views so jubilantly cited by the honorable Miss Murray from the writings of Dr. Elliott, viz., "That God cares very little for the means through which His will is working," &c.

But if God cares very little for the present means to an end, it would seem an

So certain bishops would imply,
See, gentle reader, our reply.

obvious inference that neither should man. Shall a man be more righteous than his Maker? Why should poor Hebrew slaves in Egypt—why should good and pious Abolitionists, in the days of Pharaoh—have been troubled by four hundred years' oppression, seeing it resulted so gloriously in their deliverance by Moses?

"Oh, happy sin of Adam!" says an ancient father of the church, "which brought about to his posterity the promise of a better hope than he or they could have cherished, if sin had not entered into the world." But was Adam the more justified in transgressing? If so, then prosper and cry victory African slave-pirates, Mississippi speculators, Georgia taskmasters, Virginia breeders, Alabama overseers, Tennessee jobbers, Kentucky Know-Nothings, Carolina governors! Ye Grogerties, Womacks, Keitts, Pryors, Lyonses, Prentices! proceed at home and abroad in your traffic, or advocacy of the traffic, in human flesh and human souls. Great is your reward in heaven! Great, vast, infinite are the obligations you have imposed upon the whole human race, and especially upon Africans, as the happy instruments, under those great apostles, Bishops Freeman and Elliott, of "the greatest missionary enterprise the world ever saw!"

Go on, then, ye *educators* for *earth* and *heaven!* Go on, in your own ten thousand ways, "*of which the world knows nothing!*" Go on, in your nurseries, your parlors, your workshops, and your fields—aye, from two hours before daylight till darkness and weariness send you again to your rest. Noble speculators! magnanimous traders! illustrious corsairs! chivalrous man-stealers! kidnap, separate and forever, at home and abroad, the child from the parent, the parent from the child, the sister from the brother, the husband from the wife, and the wife from the husband; ply the lash, corrupt the heart, break the back with heavy burdens, in your Sabbathless pursuit after gain—brand the cheek, crush the spirit! What is it to be a slave, if you make a man a *Christian?* What is it if ten generations be slaves, if the whole succeeding race be trained for future glory and *self-dependence?* God cares very little about the matter! Educate for earth and heaven; but take good heed that in making them Christians you seal up hermetically from their view that sacred volume which alone infallibly contains the sacred revelation of His will; nay, forbid, under the severest penalties, that they be ever instructed in the perusal of a single sentence in its pages; and that, too, while you vehemently contend that the Bible, and the Bible alone, is the religion of Protestants!

How many are there in Bishop Elliott's diocese who *will have slaves*, but not Christians! We could name scores of slaveowners in the South, who, as they express it, would rather see the devil among them than a clergyman. Nay, we

III.

The book on Parlors and on Cabins,
Though specious as the gloss of Rabbins,
On points of fact is *minus habens*,
Not more reliable than Fabens.*
There never has been, since the flood,
A slave threshed† in thy neighborhood.
Like Monsieur G—y—r—e, of La.,‡
If George, his slave, will run away,

know of clergymen who have suffered violence in attempting to impart to them religious instruction.

"My feeling just now is," &c., continues the bishop. "*Just now!*" What a significant clause: *just now*. What, right reverend sir, will be your feeling at the hour of death?

"And these," adds Miss M., " are the opinions of Bishop Elliott of Georgia! the man who remained nursing and consoling the sick and the dying, and burying the dead, when Savannah was being decimated by yellow fever, and when thousands were falling victims around him. After this, who will dare stand up and contrast his own abolitionism with the patient practical doings of a conscientious slaveowner?"

That dare we, most excellent lady; and permit us to declare, not " with self-laudatory philanthropy," but in all humility of heart, without presuming on any comparison in merit, or claiming any merit at all in a point of duty, that we know many clergymen in the South as much opposed to slavery in their hearts as your most conscientious slaveowners are in its favor, who, in burying the dead and visiting the sick and the dying, have come quite as much in contact with the vomito as the episcopal ring of Dr. Elliott.

It is but just to the bishop to admit that we believe he would, with as much sincerity as any man living, repudiate the pernicious practical consequences of the principle we have combatted. But the God of this world seems to blind him.

* Fabens, a well-known politician.

† "A slave threshed," etc.—See *Parlor and Cabin*.

‡ Like M. G—y—r—e, of La. " Did you not lately run away for two months; for what reasonable cause, God only knows, and did you not come back with tho face of a whipped dog, telling me that you were satisfied with that great blessing, *freedom*, and that you would not try it any more; if for a whole week you allow any human body to cross my threshold, I swear, and you know I always keep my word, that I'll kick you away to the abolitionists." What impression this order pro-

He threatens to dismiss *instanter*
The rascal. Creoles love to banter:
When George once took him at his word,
He raved, like Balaam, for a sword;
But, as the sword was not forthcoming,
He drubbed him, as was most becoming
In a great Secretary of State—
A man of most prodigious weight—
With cudgel, cowhide, and a rope,
Plied deftly, *à la* gantelope,*

---

duced on this *miserable* slave I do not know, but it was strictly executed. The italic characters are Mr. G.'s, and they convey more truth than he intended.— *Preface to Romance of the History of Louisiana.*

* A Western trader, captured and plundered a few years since by a large body of Comanches, and with difficulty escaped out of their hands, has described to the writer of these rhymes a discipline obtaining among those savages, which strikingly resembles and illustrates that of the gantlet, gauntlet, or gantelope referred to.

With a face much darkened by long residence in a Southern climate, and never deficient in bronze, our trader, acquainted with the language of the Choctaws, wished to pass as an Indian pedlar among the wilder denizens of the plains. While stooping to display his commodities to a promiscuous group of men, women, and children, most wistfully assembled to survey them, an unlucky breeze lifted his summer kilt, and revealed to his customers the sinfulness of his skin, or speaking more correctly, as a friend at our elbow reverentially intimates, περισσείαν κακίας. By-the-way, Robinson, after Pott, explains this phrase, every excrescence of evil, referring κακίας to moroseness in teaching.—James i. 21.

If it be true that our friend, the trader, was a *colporteur* of a morose school of theology, his pupils, it must be owned, somewhat bettered his instructions. His punishment was in this wise:

The women formed themselves into two lines with a distance of a few paces between. Our hero, in passing through this formidable Thermopylæ, received on his vicarious back, as administered with right hearty good will by these sturdy viragoes, some smart stripes, from a raw cow-hide whip, which each held in her hand. The unfeeling male savages, in the meanwhile, were jeering and scoffing at their victim.

Our poor scape-goat, knowing or imagining, perhaps, that this discipline did not fall precisely under the class of personal adventures, originating in, associated

George ran because he was so happy,
Or was it that his brain was sappy,
From cuffs and blows, which all who know
Monsieur, can prove he could bestow
On George's back, and often did,
In wanton cruelty and pride,
As we, perhaps, have elsewhere said.

IV.

Within the reach of Plodnarph's ears,
The lash each day its victim tears:
How often since the Mississip-
Pi last its grassy banks o'erflowed,
Has H—y D—l applied his whip—
If P. were frank, he might have told.

---

with, or very particularly suggestive of those "pleasures" of which a greater that Rogers has sung—

"Forsan et hæc olim meminisse juvabit."—(VIRG.)

has, we understand, as indeed it is very natural he should, become exceedingly sensitive of late, at any allusion to a *piaculum* so involuntary and distasteful. It was, in truth, a most untoward flagellation; but altogether unavoidable; or, say that prudence could have avoided, no human valor could have averted it. We offer and owe this remark as an emollient, such as it is, to the wounded honor of our friend, who, if the truth must be told, was himself—when he had power, and a black, unresisting subject—a most energetic flagellator.

Most consolatory, moreover, to a sincere penitent, like our friend, is the reflection, that the retributive economy evinced in his case and in all similar cases—how penal soever in its character—affords striking evidence even to the most sceptical, that God, as the Supreme Disposer of events, is not less wise, irresistible, and just in the moral, than He is in the physical government of the universe.

It is but justice to add, that seeing there often is, according to the philosophy of Sancho Panza, as much courage displayed in enduring as in administering heavy blows, our friend has had by universal consent—independent of the Gazette—the great solace of a brevet-majority for his passive gallantry on that overmemorable occasion, and will doubtless, in his next journey o'er the plains, go out, like Sir Hudibras, "a Colonelling!"

CHIVALRY AND SLAVERY.

That trader, planter, overseer,
Is known as brutal far and near,
As well as many more beside him,
Who, as a booby, all deride him.
Deride not P., pray mark but D——l,
Whose life is terror mixed with toil,
And carking cares and love of wealth,
Acquired by furiousness of tilth,*
Goading and driving scores of slaves
To sleepless work and early graves;
Who in pro-slavery books puts faith,
Can never clearly see his path.
One cordial drop from Uncle Tom
Is worth an ocean of such rum.†

v.

In haste his victuals to ingulf,
D. bolts them like a hungry wolf;
If chance a visitor should call,
He leaves him standing in his hall;
Or, should he ask him to his table,
He rushes to his field or stable,
With heavy whip of overseer;
And if, surprised at his career,
You seem his rudeness to accuse,
He hopes his business you'll excuse;

---

* Never in the Cabinet, the Parliament, or the battle-field, was victory more ardently sought after than it is, as respects the quantity and quality of sugar, by the planters on the Mississippi and other rivers of the South. Not even the fierce industry of steamboat hands—who, in paroxysms of effort from the stimuli of double wages and double drams, under captains struggling for the quickest passage, roll cotton bales or sugar barrels, on our western landings—surpasses or equals, in many instances, the Sabbathless toil of plantation negroes under the lash of avaricious and tyrannical taskmasters.

† Rum (Dunder) is sometimes understood to be spirits distilled from the lees or dregs of former distillations.—See WEBSTER.

He leaves you to the ladies' care,
To make the best of homely fare!
Sleepless himself, in dead of night
He creeps to see that all is right;
Horses and harness in their places,
Cows, oxen, mules, and slaves and asses;
That smell of fire or match there none is,
That in his negro huts no gun is;
Sugar and carriage-houses safe,
Hay, shavings, maize, and oats and chaff;
That fires and lights be all extinguished,
Nor the right hand from left distinguished.
Then woe betide the man or woman,
Cook, driver, spadesman, herdsman, ploughman,
That has not perfected his task,
To please this frantic basilisk.
Dragged from their beds with blows and stripes,
Of paddles or of raw-hide whips,
They glut the sordid villain's wrath,
Yet dare not cry above their breath,
Or scream on penalty of death,
Lest any neighboring planter hear,
And as a witness should appear,
Of cruelties condemned by laws,
If well-paid lawyers find no flaws,
And jurors can impartial be,
And judges charge with equity.

VI.

While often in the darkness groping,
And at some clay-built cottage stopping,
He hears conspiracy in trees,
Or in the drippings from the eaves,
Or in the whisperings of the breeze,
Or in the curling of the leaves,

Or in the marsh, or in the lake,
Or in the wrigglings of the snake;
Or in the chirping of the cricket,
Or cautious opening of a wicket ;
Or in the crawling of the worm,
Or in the pelting of the storm ;
Or in the river's sullen roar,
Or plash of wavelets on the shore,
Or in the loud *crevasse* or bore,*
Or wary dip of muffled oar ;
When by the willows, thick and dank,
The hunter creeps along the bank,
And, on the margin of the water,
A bird or stag marks out for slaughter,
In terror at the rifle's crack,
D. trembles, starts, and looking back,
There, as a statue fixed, would glare :
His blood congealed, erect his hair,
The thunder's din and lightning's flash,
He fancies as the doomsday crash,
Yea, reads his fate and hears his knell
In every tinkling of a bell,
Be it a bell of cow or sheep,
That jars his nerves in troubled sleep.

VII.

If, when his door-bell wires are shaken,
By blustering night-winds, they awaken
The restless tyrant—they appal
His guilty conscience most of all.

---

* " A tide swelling above another tide."—BURKE. Or a sudden influx of the tide into a river or narrow strait, conflicting with the water from above. Those who live, or have lived or traveled, in Wales know what is meant by the *Severn bore.*

The gases crackling in his fire,
Or insects' cries ere they expire,
Or hideous faces in the embers,
Which fancy paints, perhaps remembers;
Or howling dogs and storms and moans,
Of owls and cats and thief raccoons—
All to this wretched man betoken
Some peril near, some wrath unroken.
In flittering myriad fire-fly lamps,
He views the angels' lighted camps —
Detective hosts of heaven's police,
To guard the good, to menace vice;
In every flash some near patrol,
With lightning streak surveys his soul,
And takes inexorable note
Of every damning blood-red spot.

VIII.

Charred stumps appear as negro faces,
In threatening aspects and grimaces;
And withered limbs of forest trees
Are outstretched arms, his soul to seize;
Or ghosts of murdered souls who peal
His dirge and beckon him to hell.
With skinny lips and bony fingers,
   And hands and arms with blood begrimed;
They ask why still on earth he lingers,
   Since Satan has his body claimed?
If, when he outs his nightly taper,
A beetle creeps beneath his paper;
Or mouse should patter in his basin,
It is the knife of an assassin—
As Holofernes once was smote—
Uplifted high to cut his throat.
Not Galen's skill in medicine,

By Morpheus aided and Morphine,
Could bring to this unquiet snorer
Tired nature's balmiest restorer.

IX.

Such is the life of one who raves,
A madman murderer over slaves:
" By Heaven!" he cries, " I'll never stop
Thus struggling till I make a crop
Of sugar, heavier far than Hunter,
Or any other Southern planter;
Until I have more hands than they
Can hire, or own, or work or pay;
Then shall I live at peace and be
Indifferent as to pedigree.
What! I a Celt, my wife low Irish!
And *both* in heart and nature currish!
They lie, the knaves! that would despoil
Of high descent the house of D—l!
Ye Gods! I long with cudgel thwacks
To prove it on their haughty backs:
There's not an Ormond of them all,
So proud of his original
As I, or who pretends to be
Like me, of royal ancestry.
If they my ignorance deride,
I'll have revenge in wealth and pride;
I'll sell no more, nor buy new slaves,
They're all a cursed pack of thieves;
I'll leave them to my overseers
To manage, then adieu to cares.
I'll try to pass my latter days
As Christians should, in prayer and praise;
Like a true Christian patriot,
I'll patronize the polyglott,

And schools and missions round about,
And at camp-meetings groan and shout!

X.

My steamboats and my railroad cars
Shall all divines exempt from fares;
I'll teach my haughty neighbor Butler,
I'm not inferior to a sutler—
Or sumptuary counter-caster,
Or military Quartermaster,
Major or Colonel! I invoke ye,
His cousins! squires of Ofekenochee!
Planters of sugar-cane and rice,
Factors of slavery and vice!
Ye are my witnesses, if I
Or speak the truth, or basely lie!

XI.

If he invites me to a dinner,
I shall not come, as I'm a sinner.
What! sit at table like a mummy,
Butt, clown, or harlequin, or dummy,
While he, a mouthing politician,
At heart an arrogant patrician,
Plays demagogue or rhetorician;
Besides, I never feel so heady,
So shy, embarrassed, and unsteady,
Never so awkward and unready,
As in the presence of his lady;
This I am sure she plainly sees,
And tries to put me at my ease,
All which perplexes me the more;
For such her grace and beauty bright,
Her noble mien, her portly height,
She moves, as doth the queen of night,

Through minor stars, a mount of light—
A living, breathing, Kooh-y-nor.
No, no! I'll stay at home, I will,
And thus my projects best fulfil;
I'll build a church, and eke endow it,
Then shall the preachers, well I know it,
Who utter now such fooleries
Against my pride and avarice,
My floggings and debaucheries,
Right speedily my worth discover,
And all my wickedness gloss over.
I'll send the Gospel to the heathen,
And who can question we shall see then
My piety held up to view,
As something wonderful and new,
While all the time my life was Stygian,
As that of Cypriote or Phrygian,*
My slaves as badly used as ever,
Myself as much an unbeliever;
Yet if I now should chance to die,
And you could hear my eulogy,
Be well assured no man on earth
E'er honored more his second birth,
Or of corruption had less leaven,
Than I when thus rigged out for Heaven,
By grace converted and forgiven!"†

---

* The Cyprians and Phrygians were always proverbial for sensuality and licentiousness.

† The author of these poems has no idea that the hope of leaving a good name behind him could elicit from D. the munificence referred to. Nothing more is meant than a satire upon that bad practice, too prevalent among the clergy in the South and elsewhere, of pronouncing funeral panegyrics upon the worst sort of men—if they show or seem to show, at the hour of death, any compunctious visitings of conscience touching their past lives—or exercise any acts of liberality towards religious institutions.

www.ingramcontent.com/pod-product-compliance
Lightning Source LLC
Chambersburg PA
CBHW031440160426
43195CB00010BB/794